KT-115-913

a steroid hit
the earth

a steroid hit the earth

A CELEBRATION OF MISPRINTS, TYPOS AND OTHER HOWLERS

'Be careful about reading health books.
You may die of a misprint.'
Mark Twain

PORTICO

First published in the United Kingdom in 2008 by
Portico Books
10 Southcombe Street
London
W14 0RA

An imprint of Anova Books Company Ltd

Copyright © Martin Toseland, 2008

The moral right of the author has been asserted.

All rights reserved. No part of this publication may be reproduced, stored in a retrieval system, or transmitted in any form or by any means electronic, mechanical, photocopying, recording or otherwise, without the prior written permission of the copyright owner.

This book can be ordered direct from the publisher.
Contact the marketing department, but try your bookshop first.

ISBN 9781906032432

A CIP catalogue record for this book is available from the British Library.

10 9 8 7 6 5 4 3 2

Printed and bound by CPI Mackays, Chatham, Kent, ME5 8TD

www.anovabooks.com

For Hannah and in loving memory of Joan Toseland

contents

INFORMATION DESK

introduction

So, you're writing an essay, an email, a book, an article, your blog. You sit back, having read it for the sixteenth time and decide to commit to print, press 'send', or say, 'that's fine, let it go'. Of course, the moment you say 'go' or click the mouse, the glaring error in the headline screams at you – too late. Your stomach feels like it's hurtling towards your toes while simultaneously its contents vault to your throat. Welcome to the world of misprints. Whole departments of publishers and newspapers spend their lives checking spellings, headlines and grammar but, even so, they occasionally take their eye off the headline and allow a slip through – with unpredictable consequences. *A Steroid Hits the Earth* celebrates the noble history of the misprint.

Misprints come in various forms and guises; there are the straight typos and the grammatical howlers, and then there are the times where you really meant to delete something but somehow forgot. This book presents – I hope – a generous selection of the most entertaining from the Bible to the blog. The errors are arranged by theme and I've included some boxes of quite specific examples relating to a narrow area (for example sports shirts and Biblical misprints).

What gives typos their appeal? Typos are a form of mistake that we collect. Anne Fadiman in her wonderful collection of essays, *Ex Libris*, describes her family's obsession with typos in a chapter called 'Insert a Carrot'. In it, her mother reveals that she has been cutting out errors from her local newspaper and putting them in a large envelope for a number of years. There are 394 of various types – a pleasing haul if, as Anne remarks, one that gives her indigestion.

Perhaps one reason for their fascination is that we all do it. Even the most careful writers miss things or have blind spots; that's why publishers and newspapers employ proofreaders. The feeling that spotting a misprint (as opposed to committing one) brings on though is slightly different; in fact, let's be honest, there is not a little *Schadenfreude* (*A Steroid Hit the Earth* could equally well have been called The Book of Schadenfreude), but it is tinged with feeling of 'thank God it wasn't me'. And that's another reason why they are so appealing – we can both pity and make fun of the person responsible for the error knowing full well how they will feel when they spot the mistake.

The typo has a long and rich history. The monks may have avoided many when illuminating their manuscripts but as soon as the printing press was invented, the proofreader was born. Or so you would have thought. But in fact, as there were no dictionaries until the early seventeenth century and Johnson's *A Dictionary of the English Language* wasn't published until 1755, it could be argued that typos didn't come into existence until there was an accepted standard of spelling.

Since Johnson, spelling has become gradually more stabilized, but the earliest typesetters had to rely on their reading of the author's handwriting and their own skill in constructing pages of type in the fiendishly complicated way that the printing of the day demanded. Each letter (or common cluster of letters) had to be arranged in wooden blocks, upside down and from right to left so that the printed page came out correctly. Generally there was not enough type to set more than a certain amount of the book at any one time (a signature) so after each section, the type was broken up ready for the next signature. If the book were reprinted, the whole process had to be gone through again. No wonder then that the folios of Shakespeare are such a linguistic minefield.

But for the typo hunter everything is fair game; if the earliest examples gave us a weird array of spelling options, they also provided some pretty spectacular errors: witness the 'Wicked Bible' published in 1631 which by omitting a crucial 'not' exhorted people to 'commit adultery'. (See 'Holy Typos' p 94). In the hot metal era, spelling mistakes and headline ambiguities ('Massive Organ Draws the Crowd') of the Carry-On variety have been spotted aplenty. The linotype machine was apparently notorious at switching 'i' for 'a' and 'u'. Hence the contender for most glorious misprint of all time when *The Times* reported on Queen Victoria's opening of the Menai Bridge:

> The Queen herself graciously pissed over the
> magnificent edifice.
>
> *The Times*

Splutters of 'treason' and incandescent Victorian wrath rained down on the then editor.

Spotting 'typographical errors' soon became a national pastime, if not exactly a national sport. Corrections and apologies started to appear in newspapers on a regular basis much to everyone's delight.

The public apology masked the hidden war between typesetters and writers which has raged in the background ever since. Benjamin Franklin, the great American polymath, having been apprenticed at his brother's printers, took a lenient attitude towards misprints, being aware what a fiendishly difficult job it was (and perhaps for different reasons still is). But he is an exception. How many authors, journalists and advertisers rail against typesetters and publishers for errors introduced into their carefully crafted work? One of the most stressful times for all concerned in the production of a book is the moment the first set of proofs arrive at the author's house. Inexperienced authors invariably are on the phone within minutes of opening the parcel exploding with indignation at the 'dog's dinner' presented to them.

In newspapers, the impact of a misprint slipping through the net is more immediately felt. Here is an example quoted in *The Times* of October 1838:

> A considerable sensation has been created during the past week among the fair matrons of Wilmslow and its neighbourhood, the location of the Rev. J. W. Morris, by the circulation of a report, put forth in the North Cheshire Reformer, that their reverend pastor

> had been advocating in Stockport and urging on the
> inhabitants to petition for a taxation on wives! The
> whole village was in uproar. ... Mr. Morris was
> apprised by one of his friends of the predicament in
> which he had placed himself, and when he saw the
> maids and matrons proceeding to his house, his fears
> were excited, and, securing himself by locks and
> bolts against the injured fair, he went upstairs and
> endeavoured to appease their wrath by a speech
> from the chamber window, his carelessness in making
> this misprint. The ladies, not knowing anything about
> a misprint, separated, assuring him of what they
> would do when they caught him again on his way to
> Stockport. [The misprint was wives for wines.]

We can only hope that all concerned were reconciled once the notion of a misprint had been explained.

If authors and journalists were angry, members of the public submitting items for sale or public notices of engagement, birth or death, must all too frequently have been utterly bewildered. In the days before email, the ads were submitted either handwritten or, later, dictated over the phone. This led to often delicious misunderstandings. One of the classic examples tells a story all of its own.

> R. D. SMITH has one Sewing Machine for sale. Phone
> 66958 after 7.00 p.m. and ask for Mrs Kelly who lives
> with him cheap.
>
> *Tanganyika Standard, 26 October*

R. D. SMITH informs us he has received several
annoying telephone calls because of an incorrect ad.
in yesterday's paper. It should have read: R. D. Smith
has one sewing machine for sale. Cheap. Phone
66958 after 7.00 p.m. and ask for Mrs Kelly who loves
with him.

Tanganyika Standard, 27 October

R. D. SMITH. We regret an error in R. D. Smith's
classified advertisement yesterday. It should have
read: R. D. Smith has one Sewing Machine for sale.
Cheap. Phone 66958 and ask for Mrs Kelly who lives
with him after 7.00 p.m.

Tanganyika Standard, 28 October

Nowadays, spelling errors are less common, as the dreaded
spellchecker eliminates many of the more obvious typos. But,
hearteningly, by no means all. The beauty of the spellchecker
is, of course, that it does not understand sentences – as long
as a word is in its 'dictionary' it lets it pass. This can lead to
some terrific stories. None more so than perhaps the error on
a press release from a company that sells spellchecking
software for websites. The release listed 'the 16 million we
pages it has spellchecked over the past year'. The company is
called TextTrust, which of course you would after reading
that. The red-faced apology duly arrived, and the company
had the grace to admit its embarrassment. In the end, a
second pair of eyes is always the best defence against typos.
(Borne out by the fact that if you run your spellchecker over

the offending sentence, it suggests replacing 'we' with 'us'...)

Equally heartening is when people turn off the infernal spellchecker and let the typos flow freely. My father recently received an invitation to take part in a timeshare scheme addressed to him in the county of Berkshite.

If the spellchecker does eliminate a lot of the most frequent misspellings in published writing (although not very often in the 'blogosphere' – see below), the way is still open for grammatical howlers. Chief among these is the gloriously termed 'dangling modifier' that crops up with rewarding frequency. A typical example, taken from a national newspaper a few years ago, illustrates the point. The journalist tried to explain the various pressures on the then Newcastle United manager Ruud Gullit: 'Lying in last place in the Premiership after Newcastle's worst start in forty seasons, Michelle Cruyff is begging him to return to the Netherlands.' Michelle would be fully justified in feeling more than a little teed off to read that she is lying in last place.

These howlers concealed in the 'body' of a report are one thing, but more spectacular are the 16-point headlines that don't quite mean what they say. In these cases you just have to feel sorry for the poor sub-editor, no doubt under extreme deadline pressure, frantically trying to compress the sense of an article into a seven-word headline. It's only when the pressure is off, the newspaper has gone to print and there is time to cast an eye over the final edition that the nightmare hits home. I've included a generous selection of headlines, if only to prove that no matter how big the type, mistakes will always get through. My history teacher at school used to repeat an example of 'headlinese' to warn of the dangers of missing the big howler: 'Mayor Fights Huge Erection in Middle of High Street' proclaimed a local newspaper; whether the mayor complained or not he never said.

Other errors you will encounter in *A Steroid Hit the Earth* are corrections. These are a particular favourite. Every one tells a story and every one makes you appreciate the adage 'if you're in a hole, stop digging'.

But typos are (il)literally everywhere – from the American constitution which, depending on whom you believe, either has a comma or a smudge in the fifth amendment – '…nor shall private property be taken for public use [,] without just compensation' – to your local greasy spoon and, indeed, as the English language spreads wider and wider, to your not so local Chinese/Vietnamese or Venezuelan restaurant. I've included a small selection of menu items from around the world. It seemed unjust to include too many – typos by non-English speakers are completely understandable given the opaque nature of our spelling rules.

Other animals in the species 'typos' are the inclusion or deletion of a space in an otherwise innocent sentence (consider the effect of losing a space in the phrase 'a pen is in his hand' as actors running through an episode of *Z Cars* once did), numerical problems and the pleasing examples of appropriate names (the MP Richard Bacon calling on the government to support British Pig Farming, for example).

The arrival and massive expansion of access to the Internet has given millions of people the opportunity to have their writing published and read by the widest audience in history. At the last, vaguely reliable, count there were 1.3 billion Internet users worldwide and there are over 100 million blogs.

Some of these bloggers take their time with their writing, others don't; some clearly have their work checked by another pair of eyes, others equally clearly don't. The misprint potential is vast, but it's too big a target.

A recent report showed the Top Ten most frequent mistakes seen in the blogosphere:

> Your – you're
> Then – than
> Its – it's
> To – too – two
> Were – where – we're
> There – their – they're
> A – an – and
> Off – of
> Here – hear
> Lose – loose

None of which of course would be picked up by a spellchecker. But the joy of finding a misprint is in the fact that somehow or other it slipped through the tight net formed by editors and proofreaders.

As this book was being compiled, two friends were on a huge typo hunt in the US, travelling the length of the country, politely pointing out typos to local shop and restaurant owners. A typographical pilgrimage of sorts that is testament to the enduring fascination of the subject. Surveying local and national newspapers, the Internet, books and parish handouts from the past 500 years, *A Steroid Hit the Earth* aims to present a large selection of the most enjoyable, regrettable and bizarre howlers from the past 500 years. If there is one lesson that can be gleaned from this, it is the peril you put yourself in by committing absolutely anything to print. Whether you miss a letter, insert a space, or simply condense a phrase to a *Carry-On* level of lewdness, the scope for error, humiliation, ambiguity and outright offence is simply too wide to contemplate. The only consolation is that there is at least one person who is experiencing an equal amount of joy to your pain and anguish.

Mr Harry Eccleston, OBE, speaks at the opening of the Royal Society of Painters-Etchers and Engravers autumn exhibition, which features a special display of prints by 11 New Zealand printmakers. Mr Eccleston is president of the society and, at night, is Mrs Neil Walter, wife of the acting NZ High Commissioner in London.

TNT magazine

news in brief

This section contains snippets of news from national and local papers. Local newspapers used to be the place where all journalists learned their trade – to some extent they still are, although staff numbers are being continually cut and the news gathering and reporting at a local level very much reduced. Local newspapers remain oases of misprints, though, whether it is from the reports themselves, the adverts or the small ads you're unlikely not to be cutting something out after a skim through. Recently my local paper headlined the fact that in the Borough there were 'nore pickpockets as burglary falls'. It seems incredible that a headline with such a typo can slip through but it did and I was grateful to them.

No doubt many corrections and clarifications have been issued in response to howls of outrage from aggrieved victims of the misprints that follow (see Corrections on p49).

The Fire Brigade was soon on the scene, and once they commenced to turn their noses onto the flames the conflagration was soon under control.

Egyptian Mail

KP FOR KOSTER

New Group product manager at KP Foods is John Koster, previously with Kentucky Fried Children. Mr Koster joins the KP Nuts team and his responsibilities will include KP Disco's.

Super Marketing

The Irish Stammerers' Association will hold a seminar will hold a seminar entitled 'Aids for Stammerers' tonight.

The Irish Press

SUPERINTENDENT IS FINED

Police superintendent Geoffrey Squire, aged 42, of Brynfrydd Close, Coychurch, fined £35 by Bridgend magistrates after admitting carless driving in Aberkenfig on October 28.

South Wales Echo

'I got up and White, who was in front of me, was going to head butt me. I had had no conversation with him up to that moment,' he told Maidstone Crown Court. Mr Waller went on, 'I hit him with a fish, which knocked him back, and bouncers threw him out.'

South Kent Gazette

People in Preston ward are invited to a meeting at 7.15 p.m. tonight in St Mary's Church Hall, Surrenden Road, Brighton to meet councillors and beat police officers.

Evening Argus

DOUGLAS BADER PUB

A new public house at Martlesham, near Ipswich, has been named after Sir Douglas Bader, the RAF's legless wartime hero.

Daily Telegraph

Oxford City Council is to press the Thames Water Authority to help improve sanity facilities along the riverbanks running through the city.

Oxford Times

Walleyes Police issued the following description of a man whose body was recovered from the Mersey, near New Brighton, yesterday morning: Age between 30 and 40, 5 ft 9 in tall, good build, tattoo on left forearm of woman kneeling on a chair holding a fan, wearing dark striped suit, two print shirts, woollen vest, grey socks and black boots.

Evening Express

'It makes me want to wee, when I hear that we are getting a new nine-storey office block on the site of the old Golden Eagle pub in Hill Street,' he said.

Birmingham Evening Mail

Hampton residents woke up on Tuesday to flooding and traffic chaos when a waiter burst in the early hours of the morning.

Richmond and Twickenham Times

The new road initiatives follow a head-on crash between a car and lorry on a double-bed at Hembury Fort, near Honiton, which left a North Devon man with serious chest injuries.

Exeter Express & Star

Weather Watch

Copenhagen	12	54	20	68	C
Geneva	17	63	23	73	S
Johannesburg	9	48	22	72	S
Lisbon	16	61	31	88	S
London	12	54	19	66	S
Los Angeles	21	70	30	86	Cl
Madrid	13	55	31	88	S
Manila	24	75	26	79	R
Mexico City	11	52	19	68	C
Montreal	15	59	24	75	Cl
Moscow	13	55	20	68	C
Neasden	12	54	19	66	S
New Delhi	24	75	30	86	S

Kayhan International, Tehran

CHANCE TO WIN

Concert promoters MCP have donated three pairs of tickets for the Princes Hall show. All you have to do is answer the following question: With which band did Midge have his first number one hit in 1976? ANSWERS TO: Ultravox Competition, the 'News', 4, High Street, Camberley, Surrey.

The troops then fired rubber pullets.

Liverpool Echo

The pot growers had tapped into an irrigation line for landscaping around the gated community of Stoneridge, and had rigged up a network of white, ¾-inch PVC piping to grow the cannibals.

Orange County Register

Three farmers guarding their baddy fields in Brahmanbara were wounded by invading parrots from Assam.

New Delhi Statesman

Their range includes toiletries for men and women, a lovely selection of soft boys and a range of razors.

Evening Gazette

And a Nightingale Sang (ITV) was like a stretched Hovis ad with some real acting. Set in Newcastle during the war, it had a bravura performance by Phyllis Logan as Helen, a lovely innocent lass who falls for squaddie (Tom Watt) whose compassionate manner conceals a belief that love is ultimately just a passing fanny.

The Observer

One man was admitted to hospital suffering from buns.

Bristol Gazette

The Red Cross paid for emergency care and later found a free bed for her in an institution specializing in the treatment of artcritics.

Arizona Star

The seaman, severely injured when the ship was three hours out, was taken to hospital and the hippopotamus removed.

Daily Telegraph

The strike leaders had called a meeting that was to have been held in a bra near the factory, but it was found to be too small to hold them all.

South London Press

It was while walking home, one raw morning, from an all-night party that she caught a child.

Irish Independent

An official of the Patent Office said that many inventors abandoned their parents during the first year of life.

Surrey Local News

'So I tied up his hands and feet and got a kitchen knife to chop off his organ and bring an end to his lust once and for all.'

The man, who has not been named, was taken to a local hospital where his penis was re-attacked by doctors.

Sky News website

In many parts of Co. Sligo hares are now practically unknown because of the unreasonable laughter to which they have been subjected in recent years.

Sligo Times

She cried out in agony. And at that instant she heard a horse whisper behind her.

The Times of India

Zanuck, in his speech, showed great humility and told briefly of his beginning here in our midst. But he didn't reflect on his early struggles; how, when he wrote and wrote and got one rejection after the other and could not even get into a studio, he had to take a job down at Wilmington catching hot rivets in the shipbuilding plant to eat.

Hollywood Reporter

Dr Barrett says these lawyers are so thin that it is possible to see vertically through them and that makes them invisible from the ground, except at sunrise or sunset on clear days.

Montreal Star

Despite a temporary bitch in the opening chorus of the second act, Mr Jones earned high praise for his skilful stage management.

Review of The Gondoliers

The Ballet travels with its own symphony orchestra which is directed by Mrs Golberman. The orchestra contains 20 virtuous performers.

Clemson College Tiger

'This budget leakage is something that's got to stop,' said the President. With what seemed to be more than a trace of irrigation in his voice.

Jackson State Times

Londonderry Development Commission has plans to spend about £24,000 within the next few months on improving the standard of street fighting in the city centre and a number of housing estates.

Belfast Telegraph

But no wonder the greenfly came in their swarms (as did the audience) to hear such playing from the Royal Philharmonic Orchestra. Their technique was hot, the acoustic was dry – perfect breeding ground for greenfly as well as for the audience in the big marquee for the opening of the Folk Festival.

Cambridgeshire Evening News

Several eligible sires for workmen's dwellings, have been selected by the Southport Town Planning Committee.

The Churchillian jaw was out-thrust and the Prime Minister thumped the despatch box with a heavy fish.

Montreal Star

Winners in the home-made claret section were Mrs Davis (fruity, well-rounded), Mrs Rayner (fine colour and full-bodied), and Miss Ogle-Smith (slightly acid, but should improve if laid down).

Leicestershire parish magazine

Mrs Raymond Hackett and Miss Evelyn Fothergill gave a surprise pink and white shower for Mrs Mahlon Owens on the Ealton Lawn, attended by 33 people. One feature of the program was a Caesarian operation which proved amusing.

Vermont newspaper

During the interval the huge park was full of the local gentry that arrived in hundreds of cars and ate excellent home-made cakes under an enormous marquise.

Manchester Evening News

All members will participate in the annual club luncheon. Owing to the large numbers it is deemed desirable to eat on the first day those whose surnames commence with any letters from A to M.

South African newspaper

Mrs Thurston Longson and daughters are planning to tour the Black Hills, Yellowstone Park and other places of interest. They are taking a tent and cooking utensils and will vamp by the side of the road.

South Dakota Courier

Cash plea to aid dyslexic cildren.
South Wales Evening Post

Please bear with us while we deal with the back bog.
Letter from the Reading branch of Northern Rock Building Society

---

'You'll Never Walk Alone' (Badgers and Hammerstein)
Lance A+ sports magazine

For the flypast, four fighter jets blazed through the sky accompanied by the RAF Innsworth band.
The Citizen, Gloucester

The woman was arrested yesterday on request of Chicago authorities and is held in Communicado in a hotel.
Louisville Times

Police in Hawick yesterday called off a search for a 20-year-old man who is believed to have frowned after falling into the swollen River Teviot.
The Scotsman

Police chased the getaway cat for more than 40 miles.

Daily Mail

After being woken from a drunken sleep and asked to leave the home of his wife, the 41-year-old labourer became violet and struck out.

Rhyl Journal and Advertiser

Arthur Kitchener was seriously burned Saturday afternoon when he came in contact with a high voltage wife.

Surrey Advertiser

When the vote was called for on a show of hands Mr Newcombe announced: 'That looks pretty unanimous for strike action.' His words were drowned by a roar of protest. There were repeated shouts of 'rubbish!' and 'it's a fox!'.

The Times

Then one of the newer Labour MPs rushed across the floor to shake a clenched fish in the Prime Minister's face.

Western Mail, Cardiff

In our report of the Welsh National Opera's Cavalleria Rusticana and Pagliacci, the computer spellchecker did not recognise the term WNO (Welsh National Opera). A slip of the finger caused it to be replaced with the word 'winos'.

The Guardian

ON THE BOTTLE

A bottle of whisky and a bottle of sherry, together worth £3 16s, were stolen by a gurglar who forced a window of a house in Granfield Avenue, Radcliffe-on-Trent, last night.

Nottingham Evening Post and Standard

An item which was deservedly appreciated and encored was Chopin's Pollonaise 'Sea Minor'.

Wexford Free Press

The British and American proposals for a transfer to majority rule provides for … a constitution based on universal suffering.

New Nigerian

At 10.15 an employee of Gurock Town Council lit the bonfire and in seconds it was a flaming beacon. It was midnight before the last of the burning members was extinguished.

Greenock Telegraph

pubic
affairs

Some words are destined to bring shame and opprobrium on the writer when they fall victim to the 'typosetter'. 'Public' is one of those. The loss of just one slight letter can render a serious article meant for (ahem) public consumption to stimulate (ahem) public debate, completely ridiculous.

'When I was only three, and still named Belle
Miriam Silverman, I sang my first aria in
pubic.'

Bubbles: A Self-Portrait (opening sentence)

CUSTOMER SERVICES REPRESENTATIVES
Work immediately until Christmas. Part-time,
hours vary. Must enjoy pubic contact! Call
immediately for interview.

Ad in Arkansas Gazette, 27 November 1983

One can argue that having received medals
for heroic deeds in the Vietnam war does not
equip John Kerry to execute the war in Iraq
without seeking to discredit not only his, but
all, Purple Hearts. One can argue that the
president is using Sept. 11 attacks to bolster
his pubic profile without going so far as to
claim …

Christian Science Monitor

The latest Public Authority Standard, just
issued, is the first of a two-part set of
guidance notes on the use of lubricating oils
in the pubic sector.

Marketfact

Relieved officials from Sarkozy's ruling UMP party yesterday hoped the quick wedding and Bruni's new official status would stem his plummeting approval ratings. At 41%, they are his lowest ratings since his election – and owe much to his slowness to push through convincing economic reforms and his very pubic romance.

The Guardian

There is also the complex issue of performing for money and having the nerve to gamble in pubic.

The Guardian

We had been repressed so long in our pubic discussions …an hour of it and not a fumble.

The Guardian

Contemporary Issues in Pubic Affairs: Inside the Music Industry.

Indiana University Fall 2006 Course List

Law and Pubic Policy.
> *Indiana University Fall 2006 Course List*

Start-up, refresh, promote with pizzazz

Summers-McCann Pubic Relations
A premier wine country pubic relations firm
with extensive promotional experience in the
fields of food, wine, art, and hospitality

Destination marketing
promoting the experience
of place is the firm's forte
Getting great press is our passion!
http://summers-mccann.com/
> *Web ad for a PR company*

The First Aid treatment for a broken rib is to apply a tight bandage after you have made your patient expire.

Manchester Evening News

life & death

It seems injuring ourselves by any means or, worse, clocking off altogether doesn't make us immune to misprints. Below is a small selection of what can go wrong when you're ill, injured or paying a visit to the great proofreader in the sky. Many of the illnesses are of a particularly surreal nature, which would be hard to find in a medical dictionary.

Dr Gordon Nikiforul of Toronto University told the Ontario Dental Association that a person can help prevent decay by vigorously rinsing his mother after each meal.

News telegram from Toronto

The many friends of Mrs. Barrett will be sorry to learn that she injured her foot on Saturday. It will probably be six weeks before the fool can be released from a plaster cast.

Toronto newspaper

It wasn't the proper doctor – just a young locust taking his place while he was away.

Evening News

Doctors are beginning to accept that stomach ulcers are infectious. They are caused by a bug called Helicopter.

Daily Express

Your chance of catching an STD during your period is greater, because the blood changes the PhD level in the vagina.

More

Hooper – Wilfred Harry. Loving memories of my dearest husband who passed away 15 June. It's a lovely life without you, and sad has been each day.

Northants Evening Telegraph

OWEN. Phyllis. Six sad years today. Don't ask me if I miss you. No one knows the pain. It's lovely here without you dear, life has never been the same. God bless you dear. Loving husband, Frank.

Bristol Evening Post

Choking patients can now be incubated to maintain their airwaves!

Daily Mail

I recommend my patients eat the tables with their meat, and to be careful not to swallow their food too quickly.

Medical Weekly

55 new homes, including some sheltered homes for the elderly, are being built on this site. Access to the burial ground has been allowed for.

Putney Town Centre Plan

Mr S. Butters for reasons of ill health, is permanently discontinuing widow cleaning.

Cambridgeshire Times

The accident occurred at Hillcrest Drive and Santa Barbara Avenue as the dead man was crossing the intersection.

Los Angeles Times

Legislator Wants Tougher Death Penalty

If we are over-diagnosing asthma, then we must be under-diagnosing the other causes of nocturnal cough, such as post-natal drip.

Pulse

When Redding, a longtime scout for Playboy, discovered Smith, the model could barely right a sentence...

Houston Chronicle

The surgeon said he'd removed my momentum – the funny apron of fat that covers the intestines.

The *Worksop Bugle* recently carried a news report about a chap who'd happily 'recovered from a tuna of the kidney'.

Cutting down on fats reduces the risk of heart disease. Try to choose unsaturated fats, which are found in red meat, milk, cheese, coconut oil, palm oil and butter ...

Pulse

A transplant surgeon has called for a ban on 'kidneys-for-ale' operations.

Daily Mail

In America you can buy melatonin as a vitamin supplement. It is a hormone that your penile gland secretes when it gets dark.

Q magazine

After the morning bath take a deep breath, retain it for as long as possible, then slowly expire.

Some Chat

… she has visited the cemetery where her husband was buried on a number of occasions.

Shropshire Star

LITTLE MARLOW CEMETERY

No through road.

He leaned his head against her hair.
A wasp strayed across his face.
He kissed it.

books

Perhaps unsurprisingly the trawl for hideous errors and gaffes from the book world has not provided a rich feast. Book publishing moves at a far slower pace than the frantic sprint that is daily journalism. While the number of words to be edited and proofread for a book is huge, in recent years the daily output of newspapers can easily reach the equivalent of a 500-page book rising to the equivalent of an 800-page book at the weekend. No wonder newspapers provide such rich pickings. If you add in the amount of time an author has to write a book compared with your average journalist to write an article, then the relatively low proportion of book mistakes becomes even more understandable. But, howlers there are and have been. Here is a selection of literary balls-ups.

They danced gratefully, formally, to some song carried on in what must be the local patios, while no one paid any attention as long as they were together...

You've Got to Read This
edited by Ron Hansen and Jim Shepard

***

The old feeding of gaiety and bliss was so quick in him again that he could not control himself.

The Heart Is a Lonely Hunter by Carson McCullers

***

Over croissants, strawberry jam, real butter, real coffee, she has him running through the flight profile in terms of wall temperature and Nusselt heart-transfer coefficients, computing in his head from Reynolds numbers she flashes him...

Gravity's Rainbow by Thomas Pynchon

***

She started to struggle to her feet, with the air of her bearers.

Everville by Clive Barker

***

A shrill trumpet-call had pierced the air. It was the bulletin! Victory! It always meant victory when a trumpet-call preceded the news. A sort of electric drill ran through the café. Even the waiters had started and pricked up their ears.

1984 by George Orwell

***

Plato thought nature but a spume that plays
Upon a ghostly paradigm of things;
Solider Aristotle played the taws
Upon the bottom of a king of kings;

'Among School Children' by W. B. Yeats
(originally it was 'soldier Aristotle')

***

The Nolotic race is remarkable for the disproportion-
ately long legs of their men and women. They extend on
the eastern side of the Nile right down into the Uganda
Protectorate.

The Nile Quest by Sir Harry H. Johnston

***

Isaac Asimov collected howlers from manuscripts sent to him.
So, while technically these never made it into print, they are
too good to leave out:

Miles looked deep into those clear blue eyes who's
debts were infinite.

***

Marry me my beautiful moonlight Luna to this sun-
born, non-stop make and viola!

***

Weston was known for the firm but genital hold he had
on his men. It was one of the reasons he was chosen for
this mission over six other equally qualified men.

Thought for Today:
The whole word is in a state of chassis – Sean O'Casey

The Rising Nepal

***

'Hardened wretch,' said Father Eustace, 'art though but this instant delivered from death, and dost though so soon morse thoughts of slaughter?'

The Monastery (1820) by Sir Walter Scott

***

Heavyweights Move In – Heavyweight news on the Oxford Poetry chair front: W. H. Auden and Cecil Day-Lewis, the Poet Laureate, are expected to nominate Roy Fuller, the much respected poet (and solicitor), whose recent slimy volume New Poems was received with something approaching rapture.

The Times

For what lad can behold a pretty girl weeping for him without drying her ears on his breast.

Dorothy Dix, columnist

***

He looked at her with infinite tenderness. 'I know all about it,' he said.

She covered her face with her hands and cried brokenly. But, coming closer, he put both hands on her shoulders and lifted her tea-stained face to his.

Tasmanian Courier Annual

***

He leaned his head against her hair. A wasp strayed across his face. He kissed it.

***

Finally a gaffe from a book review – the reviewer really should know better than to be so hubristic…

It does not help if the book is full if misprints and spelling mistakes.

The Spectator

'They have been suggesting that for some time. It's all rubbish. It's fiction.' His comments followed claims that the Prince has been secretly Mrs Parker-Bowles for more than a decade, and as often as once a week.

Evening Gazette

royalty

Members of the Royal Family are constantly in the news so it's not that surprising perhaps that they have fallen victim to the misprint on many occasions. Royalty is also a subject that many people are extremely sensitive about which makes *The Times's* nineteenth-century gaffe about Queen Victoria a contender for Best Misprint.

The Queen and President Nixon exchanged gifts of silver-framed photographs during the President's visit to Britain. The Queen's gift was of two coloured autographed photographs of herself and Prince Philip, and the President's gift was a coloured autographed photograph of himself.

The woman, of excellent previous character, was bound over for three years on charges of stealing by finding.

Dublin Evening Press

Pressmen gather to see Royals hung at Windsor.

Sunday Times

PRINCE MAKES HIS MUSIC SELECTION

Prince Charles has chosen his own music selection to be performed by the BBC Welsh Orchestra for Radio Four's programme 'Music to Remember' on July 1, the day of his incestiture as Prince of Wales, the BBC said yesterday.

Princess Alex Opens Seletar Reservoir: Princess Alexandra today pressed a little button that unveiled a plague to mark the opening of the new Seletar Reservoir.

Strait Times

[On Queen Victoria opening the Menai Bridge] The Queen herself graciously pissed over the magnificent edifice.

The Times (quoted by Philip Howard, 8 October 1982)

Princess Margaret, wearing a summery yellow-ribbed cotton dress, white brimmed hat covered with daisies and yellow sandals, was shown around the laboratories.

Oxford Times

Princess Anne got a dressing gown for her recent fox-hunting expeditions.

The Charlotte Observer,
North Carolina

Henry VIII by his own efforts increased the population of England by 40,000.

Northern San Diego
Shopper's Guide

Ray Bellisario – the photographer who likes to catch Britain's royal family in off-duty poses has been caught peeing at Princess Anne's new home from bushes in the garden.

Malaysian Sunday Times

And finally, from Reuters, a story that could have been misinterpreted were you looking to do so:

Queen Elizabeth has 10 times the lifespan of workers and lays up to 2,000 eggs a day.

Due to a transcription error, an article in Saturday's **Independent** *on page 2 on Irish premier Charles Haughey mistakenly read 'a man of great rudeness'. This was intended to read 'a man of great shrewdness'.*

The Independent

corrections

Sometimes you've got to stop digging. The examples that follow all tell a story: mostly of outrage on behalf of the wronged person and Schadenfreude for the rest of us. When you're the victim of this kind of inadvertent sting there's very little you can do – if you write to point out the error, one of two things seems to happen: you either make things worse because the newspaper introduces a new error or you stir up the whole thing again and get more grief from your friends or, worse, enemies.

The fine tradition of the correction and clarification was started when General Pillow, a US General in the 1800s, returned victorious from a campaign in Mexico (although in fact it appears that he had stolen someone else's thunder which makes the following all the more enjoyable). Lauding its hero, the newspaper ran an ecstatic report of his homecoming. However, the paper's description of the General appeared first as 'General Pillow, the battle-scared veteran' implying of course that he had run away. The next day the veteran called on the editor to make an apology. What was the horror of the editor, on the following day, to see the phrase reappear in his apology as 'bottle-scarred'. Sigh. It bears out that frequently uttered proverb: 'if you're in a hole, stop digging'.

A fine tradition was born with this correction and attentive armchair proofreaders and irate victims of misprints have been haranguing newspaper editors ever since.

For many years, the corrections appeared as short, boxed articles hidden in the depths of the newspaper – the obscurity of the placement in proportion to the fame of the wronged person. The more famous the victim, the bigger the apology. Editors, having lambasted the poor sub-editor or typesetter in suitably tempestuous fashion, penned a meek and mild few lines regretting the introduction of a 'typographical error' that led to the mistake. The apology itself wasn't what made the error entertaining of course.

Nowadays, however, we have the Guardian's Corrections and Clarifications column. Ian Mayes, the Readers' Editor who writes the column, has a natural grace and humility while apologising for the paper's most egregious and comic errors. It takes the art of the apology to a new level and is the first stop in the newspaper for those who like a bit of Schadenfreude served with breakfast. Take this example for November 2001:

> 'The writer of a column about mispelling, including his own inability to spell, page 5, G2, yesterday, sympathised with Dan Quayle's "infamous" gaffe in adding an e to tomato. He did not. He added an e to potato (potatoe).'
> [Misspelling is misspelt in this correction, as a reader quickly pointed out.]

And this statement which has the ring of 'twas ever thus' about it:

> The absence of corrections yesterday was due to a
> technical hitch rather than any sudden onset of
> accuracy.

The corrections below have been collected from many newspapers and I have trawled through the archives of a number of them. Particularly appealing to me is the gracious correction of a literary critic who, according to a Times review of his *Illustrated History of English Literature*, called Byron, Shelley and Keats the 'triple freaks' of English Literature rather than the triple peaks.

In last week's issue some errors were made regarding Mrs Gilcuddy, which the following will correct: Mrs Gilcuddy was born in 1865, and was 64 years and 11 days of age at the time of her birth.

Santa Ana Record, California

Bible In Hand – Due to an error in transmission we stated in an inquest on Saturday that Mrs Susannah Vincent, of Porth, was found dead with a bottle in her left hand and a plastic bag over her head. This should have read 'a bible in her left hand'. We apologise for any distress caused to the family.

Swindon Evening Advertiser

The Denver Daily News would like to offer a sincere apology for a typo in Wednesday's Town Talk regarding New Jersey's proposal to ban smoking in automobiles. It was not the author's intention to call New Jersey 'Jew Jersey'.

Denver Daily News

Patrons please note that the 'Daily Times' of Wednesday 4 June published the name of the actor for the film Deadly Harvest as Cunt Walker by error, but it should have read Clink Walker. We regret the inconvenience caused.

Daily Times (Malawi)
(NB the actor was actually
Clint Walker)

In our issue on November 30 we reported that the Lubavitch Foundation in Glasgow held a 'dinner and ball' to celebrate its tenth anniversary. This was incorrect. A spokesman explained: 'The Lubavitch movement does not have balls.'

Jewish Chronicle

By an unfortunate typographical error in Prisea Middlemiss's article last Wednesday, Professor Ian Macgillivray and two of his colleagues were described as 'abortion obstetricians' instead of 'Aberdeen obstetricians'. We apologise to the doctors concerned.

The Guardian

BAR FOOD

In our story on London Hosts, the Grand Met managed house operation, it was stated that the 'Pub 80' concept probably appealed more to the younger drinker or those looking for bad food.

This should, of course, have read 'Bar food'. We apologise for any embarrassment caused.

Morning Advertiser

Error: The Observer wishes to apologise for a typesetting error in our Tots and Toddlers advertising feature last week which led to Binswood Nursery School being described as serving 'children casserole' instead of chicken casserole.

Leamington Spa Observer

CORRECTION

Due to a printing error, a story in last week's Gazette referred to athletics coach Billy Hodgins as an 'old waster'. This should, of course, have read 'old master'. We apologise to Mr Hodgins for any embarrassment caused.

DEPT. OF CORRECTIONS:

In that same 'Explain that Sore' article mentioned above, it was stated that a vaccine exists for Hepatitis C when, in fact, there isn't one. We regret the error, of course.

Actually, we more than regret the error. We regret run-of-the-mill errors, but this error mortified us. The editor of The Stranger, Dan Savage, is a friggin' sex writer, after all. Why didn't he spot the error? Because he didn't READ THE PIECE!

Can you believe it? Sean Nelson edited the Back to School Issue, and Savage figured he didn't even have to give it glance. God, what a dumb asshole.

The Stranger

COURT STORY

We apologise for placing an incorrect heading on a court story in page 23 of our June 29 issue.

It read 'Father headbuts son' but should have read 'Father headbuts his son's attacker.' We are sorry for any offence caused to Jeffrey Babbs of Don Court, Witham.

Braintree and Witham Times

In an article in Monday's newspaper, there may have been a misperception about why a Woodstock man is going to Afghanistan on a voluntary mission. Kevin DeClark is going to Afghanistan to gain life experience to become a police officer when he returns, not to shoot guns and blow things up. The Sentinel-Review apologizes for any embarrassment this may have caused.

Sentinel-Review

The authorities at Ongar library have received a number of complaints about a card in the index file with an entry which read: SEX: SEE LIBRARIAN. This has now been changed. The new entry reads: SEX: FOR SEX ASK AT THE DESK.

Eastern Gazette

Due to a transcription error, an article in Saturday's Independent on page 2 on Irish premier Charles Haughey mistakenly read 'a man of great rudeness'. This was intended to read 'a man of great shrewdness'.

The Independent

ANNIVERSARY DINNER

Among the special guests attending the Brecon Rotary Club's 30th Charter Anniversary dinner but not included in the report in our last week's issue was the President of the Brecon Soroptimist Club and not the President of the United States of America as inadvertently appeared. We apologise for any embarrassment to the organisers or the invited guests which this error may have caused.

Brecon and Radnor Express

Publisher's Correction, 1978 Edition of Dod's Parliamentary Companion Reference to Lord Gibson's biography on page 122: for National Front read NATIONAL TRUST.

FIT AND WELL

Mrs Rosina Harfield asks us to point out that reference to her in the report of the Braishfield football match last week was completely untrue. She is fit and well, and we would like to apologise to her for any upsets the report could have caused.

The Romney Advertiser (27/3)

USEFUL POINT FOR THE VILLAGERS

Thornhill Baptists 1, Braishfield 1

Braishfield's Saturday side had problems in fielding a team for their away match against Thornhill Baptists, and started with ten men. Mick Harfield arrived late and made the eleven, despite the tragic news that his wife had passed away early the same morning. Everybody was stunned to hear this, and at half time both teams observed two minutes' silence in respect. The idea of Mick playing was to take his mind off the matter and he was a hero indeed to stay for the duration of the match.

The Romney Advertiser (21/3)

Sir – May I be allowed to correct one misprint in my letter on the frames at the National Gallery? The original word I ventured to use to describe Suzanne Fourment's aesthetic feelings was 'disquiet' and not 'disgust' which emotion I feel sure could only be aroused in such a gracious lady by the further inclusion of a red plush mount to complete her Rococo confinement!
Yours &c

The Times

The home of Charles Darwin, author of On The Origin of Species, is Down House in Kent. It was garbled in a news report on page 12 on April 11.

The Guardian, April 21

In a correction published in this column yesterday, we misspelt Downe House, the home of Charles Darwin in Kent.

The Guardian, April 22

CLARIFICATION:

A correction to a correction of a correction. Darwin spelt, both the name of his house and the village in which it is situated, Down. The village became Downe. The house is still Down.

The Guardian, April 23

The phrase 'Dummy Head', which was accidentally printed beneath a photograph in Thursday's Clarion-Dispatch, was intended as a typographical notation for use in the production process. It was not intended to describe in any way the subject of the photograph.

Clarion-Dispatch

A caption in Guardian Weekend, page 102, November 13, read, 'Binch of crappy travel mags.' That should, of course, have been 'bunch'. But more to the point it should not have been there at all. It was a dummy which we failed to replace with the real caption. It was not meant to be a comment on perfectly good travel brochures. Apologies.

The Guardian

Just to keep the record straight, it was the famous Whistler's Mother, not Hitler's, that was exhibited at the recent meeting of Pleasantville Methodists. There is nothing to be gained in trying to explain how the error occurred.

Titusville Herald

Owing to a printer's error in the 'fairy-ring' cake recipe last week, 'two ounces castor oil' was given for 'two ounces caster sugar'. We apologize for this silly mistake.

Reveille

In a recent report of a competition held at one of Pontin's holiday camps it was inadvertently stated that it was for 'elephant' grandmothers instead of elegant grandmothers. We apologize to Mrs Helen P—, who gained third place, for any embarrassment this may have caused.

Stockport Advertiser

In printing yesterday the name of one of the musical comedies which the Bandmaster Company is presenting next week as The Grill in the Train, what our compositor meant to set was, of course, The Girl in the Drain.

South China Morning Post

Dear Sir, Perhaps you will kindly allow me space to correct a misprint in your otherwise contenting review of Volume III of the Illustrated History of English Literature. My chapter on Byron, Shelley and Keats does not refer to these three as 'the triple freaks' but as the 'triple peak'. Yours &c Mr A C Ward

The Times

The impression that the 1954 calendar of Mr Billy Graham, the American evangelist, was attacking British Socialism had arisen through a misunderstanding, it was stated last night.

Mr de Freitas Labour MP for Lincoln, said in a statement: 'My friend the Bishop of Barking tells me that Mr Graham supports British socialism's fight against materialism and says that 'attack on British socialism' is a misprint for 'attack on British secularism'. The Bishop says an apology and explanation of the misprint is in the post from Mr Beavan, of Mr Graham's publicity staff.

The Times

Due to a telephone error in transmission we stated that Mr Roger Cranwell will be knighted next month. In fact, he will be 90 next month.

There was a misprint in Mr Maurice Edelman's article 'A Firm Line', published in The Times yesterday. He wrote: 'But possessing a strong political and religious curiosity, I read with fascination the exegesis of politics which is sometimes found in irreverent autobiography, and the commentaries on religious experience by nonconformist theologians.' The first word of that sentence appeared as 'Not' instead of 'But'.

The Times

An item about a Thursday event at Diablos featuring four women DJs on Page 8 of Friday's edition incorrectly identified DJ KaatScratch as transgendered. She describes herself musically as 'transgenred'.

Eugene (Oregon)
Register-Guard

In our report of the Parliamentary debate upon the opium traffic, we included a sentence that read 'A member raised the question "How the dog was produced from the puppy?".' The question should have read 'How the drug was produced from the poppy?'

The Times

NEASDEN HOSPITAL AFFAIR

We regret that owing to a typographical error the closing sentence of Sir David Llewelyn's article yesterday appeared as 'Blessed are the merciful, for they shall receive money.' 'Money' should have read 'mercy'.

Mr Stephen Boulding, whose name was inadvertently misspelt in last week's report of the Young Conservatives' conference at Eastbourne, asks us to state that the phrase he used in mock-serious vein was 'Frogs and Italians'. Owing to an error in transmission this was reported as 'wogs and Italians'.

Sunday Telegraph

In an unfortunate error we were made to say last week that the retiring Mr South was a member of the defective branch of the local police force. Of course, this should have read 'the detective branch of the local police farce'.

Christchurch Star

We reported on Dr Luther Terry, the former US Surgeon General's advice that there should be a complete ban on all tobacco advertising, but described him as 'a smoker' omitting the rather important adjective 'former'.

New York Times

Thanks to a misprint on an anti-social behaviour order, an Alnwick, Northumberland, UK, teenager was ordered to drink in public and to act in a threatening manner.

Angered by his unruly, boozed-up behaviour, police had hoped magistrates would punish the youth for breaching his Asbo. He hadn't. Closer examination revealed that he had mistakenly been ordered not to be in public 'without' alcohol and that he was also duty bound to act in a threatening manner likely to cause harassment, alarm and distress to others.

After the boy escaped punishment as a result of the misprint, the officials behind the mistake were asked to deliver a new Asbo with more appropriate wording.

BBC Magazine

An article in Wednesday's Calendar section about an English-language newspaper in Mexico City referred to the many US ex-patriots who live there. It should have said expatriates.

Mexico City newspaper

A caption on Saturday with a picture showing a Pakistani man on his bicycle carrying a painting of his son, who he says was abducted by Pakistani intelligence agents in 2001, misspelled the name of the Pakistani capital. It is Islamabad, not Islambad.

New York Times

A picture caption on Wednesday with an article about a meeting between the leaders of North Korea and South Korea misspelled the name of the North Korean capital, where the meeting was held. It is Pyongyang, not Pongyang.

New York Times

THEY WERE NOT BORED
The title of a lecture given by William Henry Altor of New York, at the First Church of Christ Scientist, High Wycombe was incorrectly given in last week's Free Press as 'How to bore and be bored'. In fact, Mr Alton spoke on the subject of 'How to love and be loved'. The Free Press regrets the error which a misreading of contributed copy.

Bucks Free Press

In a recipe for salsa published recently, one of the ingredients was misstated, due to an error. The correct ingredient is '2 tsp. of cilantro' instead of '2 tsp. of cement'

Quoted on The Tonight Show
with Jay Leno

Mai Thai Finn is one of the students in the program and was in the center of the photo. We incorrectly listed her name as one of the items on the menu.

Community Life

March 22: 'For sale: Slightly used farm wench in good condition. Very handy. Phone 366 — A Cartright

March 29: 'Correction. Due to an unfortunate error, Mr Cartright's ad. last week was not clear. He has an excellent winch for sale. We trust this will put an end to jokesters who have called Mr Cartright and greatly bothered his housekeeper, Mrs Hargreaves, who loves with him.

April 9: Notice! My WINCH is not for sale. I put a sledgehammer to it. Don't bother calling 366 —. I had the phone taken out. I am NOT carrying on with Mrs Hargreaves. She merely LIVES here. A. Cartright.

Connecticut newspaper
(quoted in Reader's Digest)

We incorrectly called Mary Ann Thompson Frenk a socialist. She is a socialite.

Dallas Morning News

As he ran, Mourre tried to take off his white homespun sock which was tripping him, while the organist played with all bass stops open to drown the shouting.

The Guardian
(In fact, it was his hired cassock that he was trying to shed.)

A story headlined 'Syria seeks our help to woo US' in Saturday's Weekend Australian misquoted National Party senator Sandy Macdonald. The quote stated, 'Syria is a country that has been a bastard state for nearly forty years,' but should have read, 'Syria is a country that has been a Baathist state for nearly forty years.'

The Australian regrets any embarrassment caused by the error.

The Australian

And finally …

The name of this column is still Corrections and Clarifications*, although it is not immune from error as the printed title in yesterday's paper demonstrated. (*The column appeared as Corrections and Clairifications.)

The Guardian

insert a space

Sometimes a stray tap of the space bar can turn a perfectly innocent sentence into a stomach-turning typo. Often these mishaps occur in the small ads, although Andrew Lloyd Webber may not have been altogether delighted to see

WHISTLE DOWN THE WIND
Andrew Lloyd Webber' shit musical Mon–Sat eves 7.30 p.m. Weds & Sat mats 2.30 p.m.

writ large in *Thames Valley Listings* newspaper. Other examples from the world of the small ad include 'Pedigree Alsatian pup pies, price 10 guineas each', and an example that probably elicited a different response to the one intended: 'Male, 22, seeks screwing position, long cruise. Some experience. Call M— B— '(Yachting Monthly).

In the US, an event at a baseball match probably did cause something of a stir: 'David Cone's one-hitter was all but overshadowed by his rookie teammate'shitting.'

Meanwhile, in the world of television, a producer describes turning up for the first day of rehearsal for a new series of *Softly, Softly* the police drama spin-off from *Z Cars*. On entering the room, he finds the whole cast in fits of laughter. The leading man pointed to the opening line of the script that read, 'Inspector Lynch is sitting at his desk, his penis in his hand,' which in the 1970s would probably not have gone down very well with a certain Mrs Whitehouse. This is reminiscent of a newspaper that wanted to pack a long headline on to the front page but simply ran out of space. The unfortunate sub-editor took the original line – GOVERNER'S PEN IS BUSY OVER WEEKEND – and squeezed the headline into the available space with the following calamitous result:

GOVERNER'SPENISBUSYOVERWEEKEND

I don't know whether the Governor in question got re-elected.

A headline which rather understates the importance of the event by the inclusion of extra space proclaimed, 'Mujahideen seize two womens pies,' which might have been news on a very, very slow day but is hardly the story that the whole world was meant to sit up and listen to.

Sometimes a stray space can create new words and images as in the following:

> The Reserve Bank, which manages the rand' sexchange rate, has apparently decided to call a halt to its slide.
>
> *Financial Times*

And, recently in the *Guardian*, there was a particularly pleasing example following the Heathrow Terminal 5 debacle:

> Airline sources said staff had gone through the luggage system with a 'fine toothcomb' in an effort to find out what caused the collapse of the baggage handling operation and prevent a repeat of Thursday's scenes.

Whether the comb is for fine teeth or whether it is just a good example of a 'toothcomb' isn't clear

– either way I'm not sure toothcombs will be on the shelves of Boots very soon.

Two further examples show the elegant simplicity of the 'Insert a Space' category of misprint:

> And now, the Superstore-unequalled in size, unmatched in variety, unrivalled inconvenience.

> Mothers Help wanted to help with children and lighthouse work
>
> *East Grinstead News in Focus*

Finally there is the inspired piece of *Sunday Times* reporting that gave this book its title., claiming that the reason that the dinosaurs became extinct was that 'a steroid hit the earth'. Now that is a use of the space bar which throws the whole history of the world into doubt.

Sweat from the trolley

food & menus

We've all done it: sat down at a restaurant and puzzled over the extravagant language used to describe some of the dishes. Chefs and restaurant owners like to make their descriptions of the food they offer as exotic and tempting as possible, but sadly their enthusiastic vocabulary isn't matched by a similarly energetic use of a dictionary. Taking a look at what follows in this section you may wonder why they don't take more time. These *faux pas* are assembled from all over the world but I've arranged some of them into separate 'tasting' menus so that the full three-course experience can be fully appreciated. Hold on to your stomachs…

Menu 1

Starter

Shrotted pimps
Consomme with poodles
Terminal Soup

Main Course

Sole Bonne Femme
(Fish landlady style)
Veal in Breadcrumbs Friend in Butter
Quick Lorraine
(pub in Ebury St, London)
Squits with Source
(restaurant in Paphos)

Dessert

Sherry Trifle and Randy Snaps
Turdy Delight
(restaurant in Eilat, Israel)

Menu 2

Starter

Smoked Solomon
(Intercontinental Hotel, Jakarta)
Hard-boiled eggs, filled with a delicate curried mouse
(Bistro, Manchester)

Main Course

Potatoes in their shirt
Pickled pork or Boiled Rabbi
(Steve's Café, Balham)
Calve's Dong
(Hydra Taverna, Athens)
English Teak and Kidney

Dessert

Roguefart cheese

And for the Kids

Lunch of Child

Menu 3

Starter

Drowned Squid
Satiated avocados
(Peru)
Uncared Ham

Main Course

Battered Soul
(Ashoka Hotel, New Delhi)
Lamp Chop with Italian Basil
(Korea)
Mixed girrl and baked beings
Kidneys of the Chef
(Cathedral Restaurant, Granada, Spain)

Sides

French Fly
(Bangkok)
Stuffed Nun
(Royal Bengal Tandoori Restaurant, Woodbridge)

Dessert
Sweat From The Trolley

Quick Bites
Clock Mosieur
(Bangkok)
Lice Omelette
(Sapporo, Japan)

Wine List
Died Pepsi
(Cha-Cha's restaurant, Jacksonville, FL)
Pimps no. 1 or Pimps no. 2.
(Baghdad restaurant)
Our wines leave you nothing to hope for
(Swiss Restaurant)

Finally round off with
Coffee and mice pies
(St Mary Magdalene Church Bulletin, Ashton-on-Mersey)

And the best of the rest of the foodballs spotted worldwide:

LIDO CHINESE RESTAURANT

Large, bustling restaurant in the heart of the Chinese quarter in Soho. Baked crap and ginger, fried ham with scallops, paper wrapped king prawns etc. Meet outside 37 Gerard St, W1 at 7.30 p.m. – you don't have to book.

Villager

Why not visit the 'Egyptian Room'
Specialities: KEBAB, VINE LEAVES, AUBERGINES, LADIES FINGERS, HOMOS, EGYPTIAN COFFEE at the Nefertiti Restaurant …

Wine Press, Sussex University

'GROW OWN FOOD' CAMPAIGN

Mr Gregory Johnson, West Devon, moving, said we must not offer the French the opportunity to flood our market with their paralysed milk and inferior apples, We must buy British.

Daily Telegraph

PISSOLES AND CHIPS

After you have prepared your chips why not at the same time fry a couple of pissoles while the fat is still hot?

Together with some salad, cut-up tomatoes and an egg, you now have a delicious hot lunch.

When next you have friends to dinner, one cut up in a mixed salad would be plenty for eight and a novel surprise for one's guests.

Woman's Weekly

Enjoy a traditional
Christmas lunch
or dinner at

THE BULL AND CROWN

Menu
Crap Soup
or Tomato Soup
Roast Turkey with
Traditional Stuffing
Chapolata wrapped in
Bacon (ch)

Instead of mint on buttered new toes, try some chopped dill leaves; use them also for garnishing chilled tomato soup, as a change from basil.

The Scotsman

Pasta Salad mixed with either chunks of fish or baby, barely cooked broad beans, then dressed with oil and vinegar, is very good, too.

Irish Times

Handel's Restaurant
This week's speciality:
Mule's Marinère
Swindon Evening Advertiser

NAS DELICATESSEN
Learn a foreign language
Say.
LIVER PATE!
KNACKERS!
BRATWURST!
KASSELER
That was perfect. Now come
and learn about other
delicacies full of flavour and
goodness.

The mushy pees were a
delight, cooked to the point
of perfection

The Guardian

Coo forty-five minutes and
cover with a layer of sliced
tomatoes. Season lightly with
salt and pepper and coo until
meat is very tender.

Beverley Hills Shopping News

Washington (Reuters) –
Quaker Maid Meats Inc. on
Tuesday said it would
voluntarily recall 94,400
pounds of frozen ground
beef panties that may be
contaminated with E. coli.

New York Times website

**PLEASE CHECK THE
NEXT FREEZER FOR
BUGGERS, FRIES, PIZZA
& ALL BREAKFAST
PRODUCTS**

*Costright, Turks
and Calcos Islands*

INFANT WELFARE
The next clinic will be held on
Wednesday 25th January.
  The advice of a doctor and health
visitor is free to mothers and babies.
  God liver oil and orange juice and
baby foods at reduced rates are
distributed.

St Peter's Welford-on-Avon

Parish Magazine

church
& religion

The Church in its various forms and the ceremonies it performs seem to attract a more than usual amount of errors. Whether it is the sheer volume of written output describing the things that go on or whether those writing are peculiarly adept at misspelling and ambiguity is hard to say but what follows (and the box Holy Typos on p94) goes some way to illustrating what appear to be the inherent dangers of writing about religion.

MADRID (R) – Catholic nuns of the Mission of Jesus, Mary and Joseph, with a television success behind them, and Mother Superior Fransisca at the guitar, are bidding here for fame and firtune in the pope charts.

The annual Christmas party at the Ashley Street School was hell yesterday afternoon.

Springfield, Mass.

There's more to being an MP's wife than attending coffee mornings and opening fêtes, as I discovered when I called on Mrs Betty Harrison, wife of Maldon MP Mr Brian Harrison, at Copford Hall, her very English home in the midst of the Essex countryside.

Mrs Harrison is friendly, likeable, and easy to talk to. Her dark hair is attractively set, and she has fine fair skin, which, she admits ruefully, comes out in 'a mass of freckles' at the first hint of sin.

Her husband is away in London from Monday to Thursday most weeks.

Essex County Standard

NOTE

In some of our copies the article The Power of the Papacy described the Pope as 'His Satanic Majesty' this should read 'the Roman Antichrist'.

Protestant Telegraph

A service was hell at Immanuel Church, Oswaldtwislt, before the funeral of Mrs Hannah Callon, the Rev J. Beall officiating.

Accrington Observer

NEW YORK (AP) – The Roman Catholic Archdiocese of New York has joined a group of orthodox rabbits in condemning the 'Life of Brian', a movie that they say is bigoted, blasphemous and a crime.

Caracas Daily Journal

An immigrant could be rejected for any of a dozen reasons – communicable disease, illiteracy, no visible means of support or the very suspicion of immortality.

Journey to America video, PBS, 1990

Young People's Society.
Everyone is invited. Tea and
Social Hour at 6.15. Mrs Smith
will sin.

St Louis Church programme

The trial of the North-West
Synod of the United Lutheran
Church last night found the
Rev. Victor Hutchings, 39,
guilty on five of six counts of
heresy. It recommended that
he should be suspended from
his pulpit at Gethsemane
Church, Brookfield, Wisconsin.

Daily Telegraph

The Wesley Guild walk will
start from the Hen and
Chickens car park at 10.00
a.m. Please bring a packed
lung.

Pastor is on vacation.
Massages can be given to
church secretary.

Eight new choir robes are
currently needed, due to the
addition of several new
members and to the
deterioration of some older
ones.

Mrs Johnson will be entering the hospital this week for testes.

———

The senior choir invites any member of the congregation who enjoys sinning to join the choir.

———

Please join us as we show our support for Amy and Alan in preparing for the girth of their first child.

———

Scouts are saving aluminium cans, bottles, and other items to be recycled. Proceeds will be used to cripple children.

The Lutheran men's group will meet at 6.00 p.m. Steak, mashed potatoes, green beans, bread and dessert will be served for a nominal feel.

———

The associate minister unveiled the church's new tithing campaign slogan last Sunday: 'I Upped My Pledge – Up Yours.'

———

Don't let worry kill you. Let the Church help.

———

Thursday night – Potluck supper. Prayer and medication to follow.

For those of you who have children and don't know it, we have a nursery downstairs.

———•———

The rosebud on the alter this morning is to announce the birth of David Alan Belzer, the sin of Rev and Mrs Julius Belzer.

———•———

This afternoon there will be a meeting in the south and north ends of the church. Children will be baptized at both ends.

———•———

Tuesday at 4.00 p.m. there will be an ice cream social. All ladies giving milk will please come early.

Wednesday, the Ladies Liturgy Society will meet. Mrs Jones will sing 'Put me in my Little Bed' accompanied by the pastor.

———•———

Thursday at 5.00 p.m. there will be a meeting of the Little Mothers Club. All wishing to become Little Mothers, please see the minister in his private study.

———•———

This being Easter Sunday, we will ask Mrs Lewis to come forward and lay an egg on the altar.

The service will close with 'Little Drops of Water'. One of the ladies will start (quietly) and the rest of the congregation will join in.

Next Sunday, a special collection will be taken to defray the cost of the new carpet. All those wishing to do something on the new carpet will come forward and get a piece of paper.

The ladies of the church have cast off clothing of every kind and they may be seen in the church basement Friday.

The pastor would appreciate it if the ladies of the congregation would lend him their electric girdles for the pancake breakfast next Sunday morning.

Low Self Esteem Support Group will meet Thursday at 7.00 p.m. Please use the back door.

The pastor will preach his farewell message, after which the choir will sing 'Break Forth Into Joy'.

A songfest was hell at the Methodist church Wednesday.

Remember in prayer the many who are sick of our church and community.

The eighth graders will be presenting Shakespeare's Hamlet in the Church basement Friday at 7.00 p.m. The Congregation is invited to attend this tragedy.

———

At the evening service tonight, the sermon topic will be 'What Is Hell?' Come early and listen to our choir practice.

———

Our next song is 'Angels We Have Heard Get High'.

———

The Ceylon Place Baptist Church has been sold – but the congregation are still searching for someone to worship.

Eastbourne Herald

Miss Linda Ann Male, of 29 Blake Road, Bicester, was married to Mr Robert Albert Page of Stock, Essex.

The bride, an animal with Oxford University, is ...

Oxford Times

———

The police arrested two IRA leaders, David O'Connell and Joe O'Neill, after an IRA funeral later today, but that appeared to be connected to a souffle during the funeral.

International Herald Tribune

Municipal Judge Charles S. Peery who performed the brief wedding ceremony, said plaintively: 'I forgot to kill the bride. And I'm sorry.'

Tarrytown News

In 1911 he worried Mrs Laura Little of Montgomery, Alabama. They have three children.

Philadelphia Inquirer

The bride was very upset when one of her little attendants accidentally stepped on her brain and tore it.

Kent Messenger

One of the mourners fell dead at the graveside and this cast a gloom over the proceedings.

Gloucester newspaper

On Monday Councillor Thompson's son will be married to the eldest daughter of Councillor James. The members of the Corporation are invited to the suspicious event.

Suffolk newspaper

The bride wore a gown of white sheer lace with lace insects.

Cleveland newspaper

The service ended with the singing of that good old hymn: 'All police that on earth do dwell.'

Montreal Times

Spring Flowers and Egg Service Address by Rev. Edwin Strange Parents and adult fiends are especially invited.

Waveney Chronicle

An 'At Home' was held at the Vicarage last evening, the first of a series arranged in aid of the fund for providing red cossacks for the choir.

Birmingham newspaper

Britain's latest and most up-to-date atom power station has as its centre-piece a unique giant steel sphere 135 feet in diameter, constructed to house a fast-breeding rector.

Cyprus Mail

The service director said that the city had neither the money nor the equipment to restore the brides: they had deteriorated rapidly and were in need of extensive repairs.

Tiffin Tribune, Ohio

One white Rabbi, with brown ears. Found hopping on 3rd Avenue.

'Lost and Found', SA newspaper

Archbishop Sin names cardinal

Bulletin Today Malaysia

The Village Voice some years ago reviewed the play, 'Harvey', and described the lead character as being accompanied everywhere by 'an invisible 6-foot tall rabbi'.

The bride was gowned in white silk and lace. The colour scheme of the bridesmaids' gowns and flowers was punk.

Toronto Post

Traffic tailed back as far as Hemel Hempstead from the contra-flow system near the Berry Grove junction at Bushey where a bride is being re-painted at night and during weekends.

Luton Evening Post-Echo

She went on, 'I guess our marriage was beginning to disintegrate about a year and a half before we parted. A lot of it had to do with a midwife crisis because George was not working at the time...'

Manchester Evening News

Best man was the bride-groom's brother, Mr Martin Gasson.A reception was at Langford's Hotel, Hove and the couple are honeymooning in grease.

Shoreham Herald

Before a short service at Darlington crematorium on Tuesday of last week, his coffin was placed by the fireplace at the Town Hall and he was toasted by friends, family and former customers.

Darlington & Stockton Times

Ladies Bible Study will be held Thursday morning at 10.00. All ladies are invited to lunch in the Fellowship Hall after the B.S. is done.

Worshippers at a Lake District Baptist church, a traditionally abstemious denomination, received an invitation to a meeting that 'will be gin with prayer'. It won the Parish Pump Misprint Award for Best Error in a church magazine from Shipoffools.com, a satirical Christian website.

THE CHURCH BIDS YOU WELCOME

Dear Guets
You have decided to spend your holiday here in Zermatt with us. We are pleased to welcome you and wish you all a pleasant holiday. We, as your religious advisers, are ready to offer help in religious questions. The church services offer us the chance to join in united praise of Gold.

Zermatt Tourist Information

holy typos

The Barker and Lucas or 'Wicked' Bible of 1631 is the most infamous example in a fairly distinguished line of holy typos. It omits the all-important 'not's from Exodus 20:14, making the seventh commandment read, 'Thou shalt commit adultery'. The printers were fined £300 (a lifetime's wages) and most of the copies were recalled immediately.

In 1653, Cambridge Press published the so-called Unrighteous Bible in which 'not' is omitted before the word 'inherit', making I Corinthians 6:9 read, 'Know ye not that the unrighteous shall inherit the kingdom of God?' To compound the error, Romans 6:13 reads,'Neither yield ye your members as instruments of righteousness into sin …' where it should read 'unrighteousness'. Then to cap it all, they repeat the error of the 'Wicked' Bible in Exodus 20:14 and omit the crucial 'not' in the seventh commandment. The

'Vinegar' or 'Basketful of Errors' Bible was published by John Baskett, who rather sourly set the parable of the 'vineyard' as the parable of the 'vinegar' – a bad vintage clearly. In 1716, the 'Sin On Bible' printed, 'Go and sin on more' rather than 'Go and sin no more' (John 8:11), while the printers of 'The Fools Bible' had to cough up £3000 for printing Psalm 14:1 as 'the fool hath said in his heart there is a God', rather than '...there is no God'. As if God had had enough, the so-called 'Printer's Bible' of 1702 replaced 'Princes' with 'printers' in the 199th Psalm making it read, 'Printers have persecuted me without cause' – indeed, it would appear so.

It scarcely took the Rich pardon to make Cohen and others like him look stupid for standing by their man for so long. 'The moral stain of this sordid affair has begun to engulf us,' Rabbi Yoffie wrote about Rich. But then the moral satin of Clinton's career has engulfed very many people for years past.

The Guardian

grauniad

If there is one newspaper synonymous with misprints, it is the much loved and much maligned Guardian. Christened 'Grauniad' by *Private Eye* many years ago, the paper now makes a special feature of highlighting and reporting its errors in Ian Mayes's 'Corrections and Clarifications' column. Two successful and highly entertaining anthologies from the column have been published.

The Tories have been under some pressure to toughen up their party political broadcasts. Mr Heath, Mr Macleod and Mr Peter Walker accordingly reached for their choppers.

The Guardian

Owing to a typographical error Thursday's article referred to the Soviet military formula which recognised the 'futility' of nuclear war. This should have read 'utility'.

The Guardian

The influence of television in politics was yet to be seen. 'There is at this moment no politician in either party who has any real command of the medium. All one can say is that some politicians are worse than others on television: some are so bad it hurts to see them making such very public schools of themselves.'

The Guardian

American research, which is gaining support in Britain, shows that problem drinkers have recognisable habits, gulping or taking large sips of their drinks, and rarely putting their lasses down.

The Guardian

What Mrs Thatcher's closest friends are wondering is whether, as the signs suggest, she is beginning to suffer from metal fatigue.

The Guardian

For four years Sendak, a bachelor, has lived in the country, in a house dating partly from the eighteenth century at Ridgefiled, Connecticut. He walks every day in the wools with his three large logs.

The Guardian

Today's weather:
A depression will mope across Southern England.

The Guardian

The Orangemen's decision to join the second group is another severe blow to Mr Faulkner. Now he has only a handful of Unionist associations and a swindling band of MPs to support him.

The Guardian

Our story on the price of tomatoes last week misquoted Alistair Petrie, general manager of Turners and Growers. Discussing the price of tomatoes Petrie was talking about retail rate not retail rape. We apologise for the misunderstanding.

The Guardian

In 'They live by night', page 4, G2 August 27, we wrote about a man who beat bats to death with a dingy paddle; we meant dinghy paddle.

The Guardian

Are those Christians prepared to invest their money ethnically?

The Guardian

Among the most outrageous demands of employers was a request for details of one secretary's menstrual cycle so that her boss could give her a wide birth.

The Guardian

The inscribed stone found at Tintagel castle, Cornwall, generally assumed to be the birthplace of the legendary King Arthur, was discovered on the edge of a cliff overlooking a tavern traditionally known as Merlin's Cave.

The Guardian

Jill Craigie's involvement in film began after the outbreak of the Second World War, when she was commissioned by the British Council to write scripts for documentaries on Britain. In 1943, she co-wrote, with Jeffrey Dell, the feature film The Flemish Farm, a morale-boosting flagwaver in which a Belgian pilot returns home to try and retrieve his flat from under the noses of the Nazis.

The Guardian

More northern stone will be used to refurbish the original gallery's huge Ironic columns. Inside, work continues to spruce up the small but impressive entrance hall, with its reproductions of the Elgin marbles.

The Guardian

Announcing that the Hiroshima attack had taken place, US President Harry Truman explained that the A-bomb was the 'harmonising of the basic power of the universe'. The Manchester Guardian editorialised that the bombing was legitimate, but that humanity had turned one of history's corners.

The Guardian

Britain protected the Hugenots persecuted by Louise XIV.

The Guardian

Peter Thorne's hat-trick in Stoke City's 3–0 win over Bury last night confirmed the belief that the club are fast beginning to resemble the geezers of their Icelandic owners' homeland – they are building up an impressive head of steam at exactly the right time.

The Guardian

If [The Casement Diaries] had they been forged surely they would have been burned once the deed had been done, not kept for prosperity.

The Guardian

Caption: These bottleneck dolphins are in urgent need of conversation measures.

The Guardian

Railtrack was able to embark on a viscous circle of underinvestment leading to delays and train collisions.

The Guardian

[Karl] Rove found Mr Bush as a gland-handing good ol' boy trading on his family name and his charm.

The Guardian

Caption: A shot from the film Christiane F, directed by Uli Edel. Christiane F became the symbol of the mid-70s junkie generation. A heroine addict at 13, Christiane was part of an infamous group of teenage addicts and prostitutes who made Bahnhof Zoo in Berlin their home.

The Guardian

One crew member of the Winner was injured when French fired warning ships at the vessel...

The Guardian

With nine wickets down, Enthoven changed his tactics and bit both bowlers.

sports

In the hurly-burly of breathless sports reporting, journalists can get a little negligent of syntax and sense; and then again sometimes they are just let down by the typesetters. The sports pages are happy hunting grounds given that the time between the end of a match (be it football, cricket, athletics, rugby) and the newspaper deadline is often impossibly short. There is a certain condensed style that has become traditional in this genre, too, which makes ambiguity a perpetual nightmare for the average sports hack. Between trying to write in this way and having very little time to file the report, errors come aplenty. I particularly like the clearly very hurried report from the *Irish News* where the stresses of sports reporting become all too apparent.

Bedi should have been run out, but Dowe, at mid-on, misfielded badly, and Bedi regained his crease after being strangled half way down the wicket.

The Guardian

Although a huge success, Eleni admits the marathon was no easy ride.
She said: 'I was just getting over a virus and had to endure severe craps for about five miles.'

Galloway News

Godfrey had further talks with striker Peter Rogers yesterday and Rogers has now finally agreed to sing a new contract.

Exeter Express and Echo

Hampshire elected to bath first on a pitch damp on top from the early morning rain.

Wolverhampton Express and Star

Spurs have similar ambitions, and are second, one point behind Bolton, after a 5–1 home win over Oldham Pathetic.

Evening News

Perhaps twenty-four hours of speculation about Johann Cruyff's future affected the great man. Most of his dazzling runs ended with well-timed tickles.

Scottish Daily Record

Two minutes later Edwards scored his first goal for Wales, again from a corner by Thomas. The Maltese goal survived a battery of shots before the tall blind Chester centre-forward found a gap.

The Guardian

He was advised by his local caddie to take a two iron, settled instead for a tree and smashed the ball 220 yards into the hole.

Bristol Evening Post

Last time out the Armagh boys accounted for Castleblaynet and the wide open spaces of Omagh will suit their style of play. It promises toben aeentr fuck it – to be an entertaining game, which could go either way.

Irish News

SPORTS SNAPS

Stand-in: Former England rugby skipper Steve Smith replaces the injured Nigel Melville as scum half.

Daily Mirror

India were without Kapil Dev, because of a bruised finger, a legacy of the first Test, and England omitted Chris Cowdrey and fielded three spacemen.

Brighton Evening Argos

Australian cricketer Don Bradman was carried, not curried, off the field during the Ashes series in August 1938.

At the start of the race, Yale went out in front, rowing at a terrible clip above 40. It had half a mile lead after the first quarter mile.

New York Times

I enjoyed reading about the Nyssa girls basketball team over the weekend. The story was very touching except for your writer's inability to use the proper word in a key quotation.

Your writer quoted a Nyssa player as saying, 'I was balling....' I believe he meant to use the word 'bawling' which certainly has a different connotation!

The Oregonian

The Welsh international had to withdraw when the cut turned sceptic.

Preston went to Craven Cottage encouraged by three successive away wins. They finished up adding another triumph at the expense of a team considered invisible at home.

Sunday Post

The mystery fan behind the takeover bid for Port Vale today said he will pull out of the deal if his identity is revealed.

It is understood Stone-based businessman Peter Jackson wants to remain anonymous until the contract is signed and sealed.

Staffordshire Sentinel

Resisting the temptation to
shoot himself at close range,
he cleverly flicked the ball
sideways to Humphries.

The Times

Six minutes later Blackpool
went further ahead, when
Matthews saw his left foot
curl into the net off a post.

Daily Telegraph

getting
shirty

You would have thought that with the number of shirts professional footballers get through in a week or a month the clubs would have invented a foolproof method of printing the names of the players on the back. You would have thought. But, as with any printing, things happen. And it's not only players who suffer.

In 2004, Crystal Palace had the indignity of being spelled Chrystal on the team's badge on the shirts! It led to the rather surreal chant 'there's only one 'h' in Palace which would have utterly bemused visiting fans.

Victims of shirtypo include the one and only David Beckham who played as 'Beckam' during the 1997 Charity Shield against Chelsea. As you can imagine, 'the lads' had a right laugh at his expense – flashes gleaming grin. Manchester United must have a less than careful kitman as other sufferers have included John O'Shea

(S'hea) for the match against Real Madrid in the Champions League quarter-final second leg at Old Trafford in April 2003. To wrap it up United's Polish goalkeeper Tomasz Kuszczak also suffered at the hands of the kitman. This, however, is rather more understandable – or at least would have been had the error happened in the tricky middle section of the surname. It didn't – that was error-free. Sadly the man with the iron got flustered before he even got to the middle and the goalkeeper went out as Zuszczak.

Less spectacularly, Maurico Wright was rendered 'Wrigth' for Costa Rica's game against China in the World Cup in 2002. More recently, David Bentley at Blackburn appeared on the pitch as 'Betnley'. *The Sun* at the time remarked, 'If the Rovers staff struggle to spell "Bentley", then maybe it explains why Khizanishvili cannot get in the side.'

Other spectacular sporting objects that have fallen victim to the typo include Ashley Giles's testimonial mugs. The England spinner had just played the best Test series of his career and helped England to beat the West Indies and, as a result, he got the nickname 'King of Spin'. Sadly for him, his county Warwickshire decided to put the legend on commemorative mugs that they ordered for his testimonial year … only for them to arrive with the words 'King of Spain'. He rapidly became known as 'El Gilo' and crowds have been known to sing 'Y Viva España' when he came on to bowl.

Hell to pay if vicars were to go on strike.

headlines

In our attempts to be punchy, we often overlook the fact that ambiguity is the scourge of being concise. Some of the examples (such as POPE DIES AGAIN) have made it in to newspaper folklore.

CHIP SHOP OWNER BATTERED MAN
Gateshead Post

Icelandic Fish Talks – Not Likely
Grimsby Telegraph

MaCarthur Flies Back To Front
Washington Post

Steps to Help Hill Farmers Urged
Dundee Courier & Advertiser

Archaeologists Attack Dead Elephant
Athens News

POPE DIES AGAIN
(British Newspaper 1978)

BRITAIN'S MINERS to go 'full steam ahead' with next week's national pit strike ballet

Mine Strike Ballet to go Ahead

Porters march over Asian Immigrants

Liverpool Echo

Heath holds up Hovercraft

PRIME MINISTER Mr Heath held up hovercraft full of people for 12 minutes today

Evening Standard

MAN FOUND DEAD IN GRAVEYARD

Evening Standard

No water – so firemen improvised

Liverpool Daily Post

WIDOW IN BED WITH A CASE OF SALMON, CITY COURT TOLD

Liverpool Echo

PC saw man squatting on top of wife with raised chopper

China Mail

SCHIZOPHRENIC KILLED HERSELF WITH TWO PLASTIC BAGS
Milton Keynes Gazette

Heart-lung swap woman on menu

One-legged escapee rapist still on run

New Shocks on Electricity Bills

Barnet Press

MAN SHOT DEAD BY POLICE STATION

P.G. Police Say Detective Shot Man with Knife

Washington Post

Ill feeling among staff disrupts hospitals

The Times

POLICE FOUND POT PLANTS WERE CANNABIS

The Bucks Free Press

Hell to pay if vicars were to go on strike

Council decided to make safe danger spots
South Wales Evening Post

Nixon appoints FIB director
AP-Dow Jones Economist

Limb centre hit by a walk-out
Cumberland News

Something went wrong in jet crash, expert says

POLICE BEGIN CAMPAIGN TO RUN DOWN JAYWALKERS

Safety Experts say school bus passengers should be belted

Panda mating fails; Veterinarian takes over

DRUNK GETS NINE MONTHS IN VIOLIN CASE

Iraqi head seeks arms

Soviet virgin lands short of goal again

PROSTITUTES APPEAL TO POPE

Stud tires out

TEACHER STRIKES IDLE KIDS

British left waffles on Falkland Islands

Squad helps dog bite victim

SHOT OFF WOMAN'S LEG HELPS NICKLAUS TO 66

STOLEN PAINTING FOUND BY TREE

Miners refuse to work after death

Enraged cow injures house

KILLER SENTENCED TO DIE FOR SECOND TIME IN 10 YEARS

Two soviet ships collide, one dies

2 sisters reunited after 18 years in checkout counter

Juvenile court to try shooting defendant

Never withhold herpes infection from loved one

DRUNKEN DRIVERS PAID $1000 IN '84

War dims hope for peace

If strike isn't settled quickly, it may last a while

Cold wave linked to temperatures

ENFIELD COUPLE SLAIN; POLICE SUSPECT HOMICIDE

*I discovered a way to clean your oven.
Put ammonia and water in a pan and
sit in the oven.*

Dayton Daily News

instructions
& advice

This section shows what happens when you try to give a little helpful advice or guidance and get undermined by a malevolent typo or by trying to be too brief in your description. Whatever you do, don't follow these instructions.

First grease the pan with a little lark.

Irish Independent

To prevent your eyes watering when slicing onions dip them into boiling water for a few seconds.

Sunday News, New Zealand

As it is contagious you should not put another bird into the same cage until it has been thoroughly disinfected by baking or boiling.

Exchange and Mart

Lunch as Day One. Dinner 4oz lover (cooked with beef stock cube).

Scottish Sunday Standard

Small business: I am a corner shop owner in Southall. What are the DRC asking me to do before October 2004? We are asking you to find out about what you can do to make your shop more accessible. Have a think about how you would serve disabled customers – you probably have some already. Think about what you might do to open up aisles, deal with a big step into the shop or simply put a seal by the counter.

Disability Rights Commission, FAQ section of website

Add the remainder of the milk, beat again, turn quickly into buttered pans and bake half an hour. Have the oven hot, twist a length of narrow green ribbon around them and you have a pretty bouquet for your dress or hat.

Barrow News

The best pan is to hold the bottle firmly and remove the cook as gently as possible.

Women's Own

For coping with unexpected guests, it is always a good plan to keep a few tons of sardines in the house.

Woman's Weekly

Wash beets very clean, then boil. When done, swim out into a pan of cold water and slip the skins off with the fingers.

Boston Globe

The First Aid treatment for a broken rib is to apply a tight bandage after you have made your patient expire.

Manchester Evening News

Another hazard is weed killer. If wild growth on road verges looks yellow and dying at a time when it should be flourishing, the council have probably been praying there.

Dog World

**IMPORTANT.
TAKE CARE.
PRODUCT WILL
BE HOT
AFTER HEATING.**

*Advice on bread and butter
pudding packet*

**MAY CAUSE
DROWSINESS.**

*On a packet of sleeping
tablets*

**DON'T RETURN USED
CONDOMS TO THE
DISTRIBUTOR
THROUGH THE MAIL.**

*Instruction on a leaflet with
a packet of contraceptives*

**KEEP OUT OF
CHILDREN.**

*Warning on a small knife
with retractable blade*

**NEVER USE AS A
HAIR DRIER.**

*Instruction accompanying
a paint stripper gun*

**ONLY EAT THE
LEAVES AND STEM
OF THIS PLANT. DO
NOT EAT THE ROOTS
OR SOIL.**

*Warning on a potted basil
plant*

numbers

The scope for getting numbers wrong is too huge to grasp but in some of the examples below even the most cursory glance would have made a proofreader's nose twitch. In no particular order, here are my favourite number howlers. The *Pittsburgh Post Gazette* takes first prize in the 'making a story a non-story' category while Reuters' report on the effect of the Second World War could easily have been included in 'Rewriting History' (see p143).

Snooker table, 88ft x 4ft, slate bed.

Exeter Express and Echo

Families with, in all, more than 500,000 children to be better off as from next August through the family income supplement, some by as much as £3 per week.

Oldham Evening News (BBB31)

Please read in paragraph nine: 'about 27 million Soviet citizens died' … instead of … 'more than 27 Soviet citizens died'.

Reuters

The tornado, which lasted only 5 minutes and blew at an estimated speed of 9 miles an hour, caused property damage running into the hundreds of thousands of dollars. Property damage in Washington may reach more than $000,000, it is estimated. Navy officers estimate damage to the air station at a sum between $00,000 and $000,000. Alexandria's property damage is estimated at $00.

Pittsburgh Post Gazette.

IN AN ITEM in yesterday's paper on how Kirstie Alley lost 75 pounds, it was incorrectly stated that she 'ate … Twenty-six, seven, eight thousand calories a day'.
The correct figures are six, seven, eight thousand calories a day.

New York Daily News

Chocolate potato cake: 6oz margarine, 1oz cocoa, 4oz mashed potato, 5oz self-raising flour, 433 eggs, size 3.

Woman's Weekly

A detached 213 bedroomed bungalow on large corner plot.

South Wales Echo

Heather Mills's charitable donations, recorded in the part of the divorce case judgment released to the public, are £627,000 and not £627.

The Guardian

In one edition of today's Food Section, an inaccurate number of jalapeño peppers was given for Jeanette Crowley's Southwestern chicken salad recipe. The recipe should call for two, not 21, jalapeño peppers.

Applications for membership now being
accepted for the Candlelight Room. A discreet
Discotheque for the over 215's.

Northampton Evening Telegraph

Talks about the constitutional means of transferring power to Franco's heir, 37-year-old Prince Juan Carlos, were suspended when the deterioration in the Caudillo's condition became plain. Franco slipped towards death with the supreme poker he had exercised for 36 years still clutched between his hands.

The Observer

rewriting history

Sometimes misprints make us reassess what we know or suspected happened many years ago. The following examples certainly throw new light on our understanding of events and people in the past.

His cautious words were obviously directed at critics in America – particularly in Congress – who think he and Dr Kissinger have given too much ground to humour the Russians in agreeing to sing the 30,000 word Helsinki declaration this week.

Sunday Telegraph

***

Papers in Iran headlined the deal not as a compromise but as a victory. 'It's over. The Great Stan bows to our demands', said the newspaper Ka Han, using the term used by Iranian officials to describe the United States.

Daily Telegraph

***

A front-page article yesterday about the role that Barack Obama's wife, Michelle, is playing in his presidential campaign rendered incorrectly a word in a quotation from Valerie Jarrett, a friend of the Obamas who commented on their decision that he would run. She said in a telephone interview, 'Barack and Michelle thought long and hard about this decision before they made it' – not that they 'fought' long and hard.

New York Times

The skeleton was believed to be that of a Saxon worrier.

Express and Echo

***

On April 14, a group of some 1,500 Cuban mercenaries and counter-revolutionaries supported by the United States and its notorious clock-and-dagger arm, the CIA, failed completely in an attempted invasion of Cuba at the Bay of Pigs.

Daily News, Dar Es Salaam

***

Heavy overnight fishing in El Salvador's strategic southeastern Unsulutan Province was reported by military sources Monday as left-wing guerrillas switched the focus of their attacks from the north.

Athens News

To finance all these activities, Mr Brezhnev does not need to hide away and misuse odd sums from party funds: a large slice of the whole Soviet national income is freely available, and freely used. The opening of mail and tapping of telephones are taken for granted, as is the concealing of listening devices. Mr Brezhnev's political police are positively obsessive buggers.

The Economist

***

In the United States, four Libyan diplomats accused of intimidating Libyan dissidents are being recalled under an agreement reached between Washington and Tripoli.

It was reported yesterday that Scotland Yard strongly murdered two opponents of Colonel Qadhafi in London.

The Observer

***

Naval elements of Iran's Revolutionary Guard equipped with high speed lunches are based on the nearby island of Larak, now Iran's main oil terminal.

The Observer

WASHINGTON – On orders from the White Mouse, the FBI last night sealed off the offices of the ousted special Watergate prosecutor Archibald Cox and his staff.

International Herald Tribune

***

Many of those arrested [in South Africa] in connexion with the treason allegations were wearing small flags bearing the words 'Forward to Freedom'. Because of a misprint some of the flags said 'Freedom to Freedom'.

The Times

***

Alan Greenspan in hospital for an enlarged prostitute.

ABC TV News caption

HALF PENNY'S EXIT

London, June 26 (Reuter) – Britain has ceased minting the half-pinny, the lowest value coin in the currency, Chancellor of the Exchequer, Roy Jenkins told Parliament.

Queen Elizabeth yesterday made a proclamation calling in all help-pinnies by July 31 after which they would not be legal tender, Mr Jenkins said.

It is estimated that there are about 980 million helf-pennies in circulation.

Today virtually nothing can be bought for a help-penny, twice the value of the now-abolished farthing.

Times of India

***

Before taking a glimpse at T5, take students back to the beginnings of London's main airport. Some fascinating film footage from 1949 shows the intensive manual labour that built the first runways, the rather gentile first travellers, and pavilion tents serving as terminals as the airport rose out of a grass airstrip during the war years.

The Guardian

A decade later, Shakespeare had so invaded, colonised and coloured Collins' subconscious that, when called upon to say a few words to the troops on the eve of invading Iraq, he spoke in the plain, unvarnished voice of Henry V at Agincourt. With some biblical additions of his own. It was 'Cry God for Harry, England and the Saint James version!'

The Guardian

***

In our obituary of Thomas Ferebee, page 22, yesterday, we said that President Truman had described the A-bomb as the 'harmonising of the basic power of the Universe'. He said 'the harnessing of the basic power of the Universe'.

The Guardian

***

... the World War II British general whose forces defeated the Italians in Ethiopia and Eritrea and restored Haile Selassie to his throne, in Tunbridge Wells, England.

The Spokesman, Spokane, Washington

Mr Winsor's other missive yesterday was an attempt to put the brakes on Notwork Rail, whose annual spending he wants down from £6 billion to £4 billion within five years.

Daily Telegraph

names

Not all of these are actually misprints, but those that aren't are simply too attractive to pass over. So when you have an MP called Bacon sponsoring a bill for the British pig industry the scissors come out. Sometimes one wonders whether a person's name dictates their thinking about their chosen career (the clairvoyant Mr Deadman for example); and sometimes perhaps the sub-editor or journalist is just being a little playful (Bishop Banana denying a split).

National Tyre Service has announced the appointment of F G Skidmore as general manager of its garage equipment company based in Northampton.

Both Bishop Muzorewa and Banana have denied any split.

The Guardian

A cross party Early Day Motion tabled by British pig industry supporter Richard Bacon MP – Tory MP for South Norfolk – will also call for the government's support for British pig farming.

BBC News website

He and his wife Gillian, who is a teacher, have three children, Gaven aged 13 and 11-year-old twins ugh and Helen.

Orpington News Shopper

Letchworth Spiritualist Church, Gernon Walk
An evening of Clairvoyance with Mr Deadman Saturday, July 27, at 7.00 p.m.

Stevenage Express

He said both assailants were white, aged about 22, and one had a large 'buzzard-like' nose.

Witnesses should contact Mr Bird, of Hornchurch CID.

Romford Recorder

BONE-MARROW – The engagement is announced between Joanne Louise, only daughter of Mr and Mrs. D. Marrow, *** Bury Road and Kevin James Bone, only son of Mr and Mrs J. Bone.

Bury Times

A talk on guide dogs for the blind will be given at Brazley Library, Cedar Avenue, Horwich, on Monday at 7.30 p.m. The talk will be given by Mrs Wooff.

Bolton Journal

HOUSE OF COMMONS
(Services) Library Sub-Committee Committee Clerk Mr Pamphlett

Vacher's Parliamentary Companion

MARY NUTTER
Psychometry, Tarot, Healing Whatever your problem I can give you Psychic Advice from your letter
But if you don't really want the truth, don't waste your money or my time
Fee £2 per question

Absent Healing Free

Plus s.a.e. to Box 29 c/o Prediction

Prediction Magazine

WILD TALK
The Wandsworth branch of the London Wildlife Trust has organised a talk on 'Gardens for Wildlife'. Mrs Robin Robins will be speaking about London wildlife at the Northcote library in Battersea on 18 April at 7.30 p.m. For further details phone …

Streatham and Tooting News

LADY WANTED in our
Garment Rental Department
No Experience
Full or Part-Time
Please apply to Mr R. Niker
JACK O'NEWBURY
QUEEN'S ROAD
NEWBURY

Newbury Weekly News

I, Sandra Short, hereby give
notice that I have, as from
February 25, 1982,
renounced my former name
and have as from February
25, 1982, assumed the name
of Sandra Long.

The Guardian

BEES BILL
[THE LORD AIREDALE in
the Chair].
Clause 1 (Control of pests
and diseases affecting bees):
Lord HIVES moved
Amendment No 1.

Hansard

With the Chief Constable will
be Division Commander
Chief Supt Peter Skinner,
and Chief Inspector G.
Bollard of the traffic division.

Buckingham Advertiser

We apologise for a
typographical error which
changed the Muttahida
Quami Movement to the
'Muttonhead Quail
Movement'.

Reuters

The women's a cappella
group to which we intended
to refer on page 13 of the
Guide (North edition),
March 25, under Liverpool-
Merseyside Festival is Soul
Purpose, not Foul Purpose

The Guardian

rude

Those of a nervous disposition and offspring of Mary Whitehouse look away now. Sometimes a typo or a mangled headline just is obscene – one can't do anything about it, it just is. Here is a small selection.

> Dressed in an ash suit and wearing the familiar red rose in his bottom hole, Lt General Afrifa appeared for the last time.
>
> *Pioneer, Ghana*

> In attempting to defend his stand BHUTTO EXPOSES HIMSELF.
>
> *Sunday Standard, India*

A period of time was needed before African
majority rule could take over in Rhodesia.
'And the time required cannot be measured
by cock or calendar, but only by achievement.'

Middlesborough Evening Gazette

This is some slogan:

In order to better the service and the
welcome given to tourists that visit Spain, the
Secretariat of State for Tourism is
undertaking a publicity campaign, which, with
the slogan 'Tourism benefits everyone, take
care of tit', hopes to increase the attention
and affability given to the tourist not only by
the professionals who work in this sector but
also by the public in general.

Spanish Tourist Office information

Anyone who does not apply research to the original appreciation of the situation and to the assessment of results is behaving like a blind man with neither a white stick nor a guide dog.
Yet management and clients do put their penises in blind men's begging bowls.

Frank Jefkins, Principal. Frank Jefkins School
of Public Relations

Finally a headline that someone really ought to have looked at twice:
PRO BALLER DIES IN BED

Dover Road: Semi-det. House with sea through lounge.

Folkestone, Hythe and District Herald

adverts

Over the years, the small ads and classifieds have proved fertile hunting grounds for misprint spotters. A lot of this derives from the fact that these ads were often phoned in or, before that, submitted on a handwritten form. In their desire to keep the word count (and therefore cost) down to a minimum, advertisers also compressed sentences with gratifyingly ambiguous results.

LOST

Lost Ashcroft/Grange Park, Small kitten – grey tabby with white chest, stomach & feet missing since Easter Monday, Please contact: —

South Somerset Advertiser

Children shot for Christmas in the home – Regent Studios

Morecambe Visitor

CHEAPEST SHAG IN LEEDS FOAMBACKED 4 FANTASTIC COLOURS

Leeds Evening Post

MOBILE SNACK BAR

(Transit) Fitted with griddle, hit dog unit, cooker, twin sinks, boiler. In lovely condition. A real bargain. MOT £845 o.n.o

Beds & Bucks Observer

PROFESSIONAL 29 years, Asian, gentleman, seeks female frieds (plutonic), any nationality for socialising and evenings out. Box 28B.

Ms London

ONE ORGASM BAG, colour tan £5

Bury Free Press

LESBIAN, 35, non-smoker, loves horses seeks same for friendship

Spare Rib

FOUND Tuesday, 26 February, black and white female kitchen wearing collar – Apply 8 Mafeking …

Champion Shopper

THOROUGHBRED FILLY, 2 years old, for sale, by Shit in the Corner out of Lady Dromara. Approximately 15.2 years old …

Dumfries and Galloway Standard

I'm looking for a kind home for my 15.1 heavyweight Cob Gelding, he's quiet in every way, but gay. £700 o.n.o.

Western Morning News

GUERNSEY cow, freshly carved, quiet, used to being hand milked.

Haslemere Herald

PART-TIME DENTON HALL & BURGIN SOLICITORS SEEK A POOF READER for their Word Processing Department.

Evening Standard

NATURIST MALE, 38, seeks lady to accompany him on trips. She should be uninhabited and adventurous.

Hitchin, Letchworth and Baldock Herald

SUCCESSFUL businesswoman, widower, aged 44, usual trappings, non-smoker with varied interests, seeks affectionate, understanding female to shave the enjoyable things in life. Box No—

Yorkshire Post

PLEASE save from destruction, three kitchens in desperate need of good caring homes.

South Wales Evening Post

MEMSAHIB Our food must be good: 20,000 flies can't be wrong

22 Upper Richmond Road, East Putney SW15

WIDOW CLEANERS REQUIRED on large contract for Saturday work, experienced on ladders and with Squeegees.

Waltham Forest Extra

DO YOU SCRATCH YOUR BOTTOM WHILE TAKING A BATH? Have it reglazed by the professional. Tel 447 —

Edinburgh Advertiser

INVALID chair, 'Dudley Extra plus Electronic' complete with lights, indicators and safety belt, has substantial kerb-crawling facility, necessary batteries and battery charger, excellent condition, paid £1,900, for sale at £1,199 o.n.o.

Harrogate Champion Shopper

Reliable person required until end July to surprise 2 boys after school in home in Crabbet Park estate – Crawley 88— evenings.

The Herald

LODGE, WESTERN HIGHLANDS

20 August–2 September Fully furnished, sleeps 8 Grouse, 4 stags, ptarmigan trout. £980 + VAT.

The Times

DOG KENNEL, suit medium sized dog. Good condition. Very turdy. Buyer collects. £9.99.

Wisbech Standard

FINE FURS BY AUCTION

Superb natural Russian sable maxi coat by Herbert Duncan: exceptionally fine lynx, cheetah, fox, mink etc. together with every type of fur in all price ranges.

MARCH 24 AT 11.00 A.M. ON VIEW.

PHILLIPS Fine rat auctioneers
7 Blenheim Street

FOR SALE:
83 Ford Grandad.

Express and Star,
Wolverhampton

BRINKS 'Open Hearth' stove

There is nothing as cosy as a Brink open hearth. Used either as an open fire or as a stove, it takes coal, wood, anthracite or Coalite, and brings back almost forgotten feelings of well-being during the long and chilly winter evenings.

Although from a finer mould, but just as strong and robust as the series bigger Brink stoves, this stove is particularly suited to smaller rooms.

It has two plates on top that provide economical and practical comfort.

A singing cattle and an inviting pot of fresh coffee bring back the nostalgic atmosphere of old.

And what could be nicer than to spend a happy hour after school gathered around the glowing stove with children having a nice cup of steaming chocolate.

Advertising Leaflet

WIDOWER, 52, a lonely and sincere genuine man who is certainly not at the pope and slippers stage of life.

Toowoomba, Queensland Chronicle

LABRADOR PUPPIES. Black & yellow. Parents hip & eye tested. Dad elbow scored. Mum family poet.

Monthly Advertiser

WALTER, 56, slightly disabled, seeks sex with men of any age. Must be hairy around Walsall area.

Manzone

EXPERIENCED NANCY

with excellent housekeeping skills & high standards seeks position.

The Scotsman

LADY, reasonable looks, medium build, 65, like short walks, outings, the occasional drunk.

Westmorland Gazette

LOVING FEMALE, 49, slim/medium build, many interests, seeks that special, kind, caring, honest, gut to share life with.

Hull Daily Mail

WEDDING AT ST MARY'S CHURCH. Captain B— to Violent Vera, daughter of Mr and Mrs J.B.L—

Calcutta Post

Cat carrying basket urgently required.

Heaton Chapel Guardian

AIREDALES – house-trained, safe with children, best protection against burglars or ladies living alone.

Dog World

WANTED – Man to take care of cow that does not smoke or drink.

The Pickens Sentinel

COMPLETE HOME FOR SALE; two double, one single bed, dining-room, three-piece suite, wireless, television, carpets, lion etc.

Portsmouth Evening News

The outbuildings include a heated greenhouse and a petting shed

A C Frost and Co (estate agent's blurb)

FERRARI …expensive mechanical overhaul, discs, humorous expensive extras.

Exchange & Mart

At Southbourne, well-built detached house in sheltered position yet with sea views, adjoining bus route and short walk to shops. Immediate possession. 3 good bedrooms and two spacious deception rooms.

Bournemouth Evening Echo

LOST
Antique Cameo ring, depicting Adam and Eve in Market Square Saturday night.

Essex newspaper

FOR SALE: A rarely comfortable modern detached residence.

Irish Times

FUR COAT, the property of a lady chauffeur, real minx.

CLOTHES BRUSH. The genuine pigskin back opens with a zipper and inside are tweezers scissors, nail-file and a bomb.

Canadian newspaper

COPY TYPISTS require work at home. Anything awful considered.

Rochdale Observer

JUST OUT. Revised and enlarged Rules of Punction. A valuable, easy-to-understand text for secretaries, writers, and students. For a free copy send a stamped self-addressed envelope. Ask for Punciation pamphlet.

Indiana News

Capitalist will consider financing Canadian oil fields or will send English theologist to investigate property.

Evening Standard

SAFE AND WARM. Make sure you and your family are safe and warm from carbon monoxide poisoning.

British Gas ad

LARGE TRUNK, can be locked, ideal for student. £16.

Northern Echo

COLLAPSIBLE BED

ideal for guests.

Buckingham Advertiser

A bath, late Victorian, as used by chartered accountant with clawed feet. Offers.

Hampstead and Highgate Express

Electric carving knife, brand new, £4. Other baby toys at various prices.

Sutton Herald

Brand new three pink bridesmaids, dresses plus accessories. £35 each.

Wimbledon Guardian

Car Boob Sale.

West Sussex free paper

MALE (24) seeks doom in central flat. Please phone ...

Edinburgh Evening News

**SOMERSET COUNTY
COUNCIL EDUCATION
DEPARTMENT
SEXEY'S SCHOOL,
BRUTON**

ASSISTANT
COCK

Required immediately.
The salary for this 40
hours per week post
will be based on an
hourly rate of ...

The Western Gazette

B— & SONS, Home-
Decorators and plumbers
etc. All work cheaply and
nearly done.

Perthshire Advertiser

PALACE. S cc 01-437-6834.
From Sept 17, The Fabulous
New Production of
OKLAHOMO!

The Times

**LEWISHAM LEISURE
CENTRE** is about to launch
a new set of courses.

Each of the weekly courses
– all but one containing sex
sessions – begins at the
centre in Rennell Street in
September.

Lewisham Outlook

**CENTRAL OTAGO STUD
FARM** requires SINGLE
YOUNG MAN

23rd August–11 September 9.00 a.m. Daily except Saturdays. Finals held on Friday of each week. GREAT YARMOUTH OPEN BOWELS FESTIVAL Great Yarmouth Bowling Greens, Marine Parade

---

Britain's latest magazine for women is looking for fast, accurate sub-editors who can turn out bright copy without forgetting to cross the i's and dot the t's.

UK Press Gazette

ROTHERHAM METROPOLITAN BOROUGH COUNCIL.

Crematorium assistant required. The Council operates a no-smoking policy.

Sheffield Star

LAKER AIRWAYS requires Cabin Staff. All applicants must be between 20 and 33 years old. Must be able to swim.

Daily Mail

DARLINGTON AMATEUR OPERATIC SOCIETY.

Booing office opens on Monday.

Darlington & Stockton Times

THE MILLINERY DEPARTMENT will be on the second floor and the proprietor states that their aim will be to always have the latest and last word in women's hats at appalling prices.

Union City Times, Indiana

ILLITERATE? Write today for free help.

AUTO REPAIR SERVICE. Free pick up and delivery. Try us once, you'll never go anywhere again.

3-YEAR-OLD TEACHER NEEDED for pre-school. Experience preferred.

MIXING BOWL set designed to please a cook with round bottom for efficient beating.

FOR SALE: an antique desk suitable for lady with thick legs and large drawers.

NOW IS YOUR CHANCE to have your ears pierced and get an extra pair to take home too.

WE DO NOT TEAR YOUR CLOTHING WITH MACHINERY. We do it carefully by hand.

FOR SALE: Three canaries of undermined sex.

VACATION SPECIAL: have your home exterminated.

MT KILIMANJARO, the breathtaking backdrop for the Serena Lodge. Swim in the lovely pool while you drink it all in. The hotel has bowling alleys, tennis courts, comfortable beds, and other athletic facilities.

GET RID OF AUNTS. Zap does the job in 24 hours.

TOASTER: a gift that every member of the family appreciates. Automatically burns toast.

FOR RENT: 6-room hated apartment. Man, honest. Will take anything.

USED CARS: why go elsewhere to be cheated. Come here first.

CHRISTMAS TAG-SALE. Handmade gifts for the hard-to-find person.

OUR BIKINIS ARE EXCITING. They are simply the tops.

SKI – SAAS FEE, VERBIER. Mixed parties in chalets bang on slopes, 21 Dec.

The Guardian

S. Paroskos and Helen
Walker would like to
announce that they are no
longer engaged.

ENGAGEMENTS.
Paroskos of Paphos,
Cyprus, and Nicola Jared
of UK would like to
announce their
engagement.

Cyprus Weekly

top ten misprints

A Steroid Hit the Earth celebrates many typographical achievements – from the extraordinary headline to the riveting small ad – here is a personal selection of favourites.

1) R.D. SMITH has one Sewing Machine for sale. Phone 66958 after 7.00 p.m. and ask for Mrs Kelly who lives with him cheap.

Tanganyika Standard, 26 October

R. D. SMITH informs us he has received several annoying telephone calls because of an incorrect ad. in yesterday's paper. It should have read: R.D. Smith has one sewing machine for sale. Cheap. Phone 66958 after 7.00 p.m. and ask for Mrs Kelly who loves with him.

Tanganyika Standard, 27 October

R.D. SMITH. We regret an error in R.D.
Smith's classified advertisement yesterday. It
should have read: R.D. Smith has one Sewing
Machine for sale. Cheap. Phone 66958 and ask
for Mrs Kelly who lives with him after 7 p.m.

Tanganyika Standard, 28 October

2) OWEN. Phyllis. Six sad years today. Don't
ask me if I miss you. No one knows the pain.
It's lovely here without you dear, life has
never been the same. God bless you dear.
Loving husband, Frank.

Bristol Evening Post

3) The Orangemen's decision to join the
second group is another severe blow to Mr
Faulkner. Now he has only a handful of
Unionist associations and a swindling band of
MPs to support him.

The Guardian

4) P.G. Police Say Detective Shot Man with
Knife.

Washington Post

5) Mr Winsor's other missive yesterday was an attempt to put the brakes on Notwork Rail, whose annual spending he wants down from £6 billion to £4 billion within five years.

Daily Telegraph

---

6) Mr Harry Eccleston, OBE, speaks at the opening of the Royal Society of Painters-Etchers and Engravers autumn exhibition, which features a special display of prints by 11 New Zealand printmakers. Mr Eccleston is president of the society and, at night, is Mrs Neil Walter, wife of the acting NZ High Commissioner in London.

TNT magazine

---

7) Police in Hawick yesterday called off a search for a 20-year-old man who is believed to have frowned after falling into the swollen Rever Teviot.

The Scotsman

8) Heavy overnight fishing in El Salvador's strategic southeastern Unsulutan Province was reported by military sources Monday as left-wing guerrillas switched the focus of their attacks from the north.

Athens News

9) WASHINGTON – On orders from the White Mouse, the FBI last night sealed off the offices of the ousted special Watergate prosecutor Archibald Cox and his staff.

International Herald Tribune

10) 'They have been suggesting that for some time. It's all rubbish. It's fiction.' His comments followed claims that the Prince has been secretly Mrs Parker-Bowles for more than a decade, and as often as once a week.

Evening Gazette

Sources

A quick note on sources. Where possible I have given the publication (newspaper, magazine or website) in which the misprint occurred. Where this is not possible I have included the misprint anyway without a source. If anyone has a source for a misprint or would like to send me their own examples then please do contact me at asteroidhittheearth@googlemail.com.

Acknowledgements

Thanks to Tom Bromley and Mal Croft at Portico for their patience, advice and enthusiasm (and also, Mal, for the Badhdad headline). I've benefitted from contributions, advice and help from lots of people but particularly thanks to: Keith Taylor, Bela Cunha, John Perry, Cathy and James, Robin Lough, Simon and Kim and Dad.

Martin Toseland
May 2008

The Edn